The Excellencies of Musick

Highlights from the
Jamie and Michael Kassler Collection

NATIONAL LIBRARY
OF AUSTRALIA
PUBLISHING

Foreword

This book and exhibition celebrate both the long association of the National Library of Australia and Drs Jamie and Michael Kassler, and their very generous gifts to the Library.

The Kasslers' relationship with the National Library of Australia began in the 1970s and has developed and strengthened, encompassing many former and current staff members. The relationship became a philanthropic one in the 2000s, when the Kasslers began the process of donating material to the Library. In 2024, the collection consists of nearly 1,800 individually catalogued titles, in addition to several collections of papers. The collection is growing every year.

In the late 2010s, the Kasslers agreed to fund a three-year curatorial position at the Library with a remit to research and promote the Library's Rare Books and Music collections up to 1840. Dr Susannah Helman occupied this role from September 2021 to December 2024, sharing her research on the Library's collections widely through blogs, events and conference papers. She also contributed to the curatorial collection development work of the Library. The Kasslers' support facilitated national and international travel to represent the Library at Australian rare books fairs and rare books and music conferences, a rare books conference in New Zealand, two courses at the London Rare Books School, research in the United Kingdom and France and meetings with local and international specialists.

Susannah curated the current exhibition, which features the items explored in this book, here described by the collectors themselves. Susannah's essay shows how the Kassler Collection complements and enriches the Library's holdings. Further information about the exhibition is available through the Library's website.

We are very grateful for the Kasslers' long-term support for the Library, contribution to this publication, and their thoughtfulness and dedication in sharing their knowledge and collections so generously with the nation.

Dr Marie-Louise Ayres FAHA
Director-General, National Library of Australia

About Our Collection

We decided to form our collection of books, manuscripts, music, portraits and ephemera shortly after our marriage. Both of us had studied music history and music theory at university, and we wanted to continue our research in that field and to publish books and articles about our findings. When we moved to Australia 50 years ago, most of the source material we needed to examine was unavailable in libraries, which meant we had to try to acquire these items ourselves. Our quest was aided by frequent trips to bookshops in the United Kingdom and the United States of America, where, unlike today, many of the items we sought could still be bought at affordable prices.

The present exhibition contains works relating to music that were printed or handwritten in the United Kingdom between 1636 and 1850. It showcases a very small portion of our collection, which now comprises more than 3,000 works on multiple subjects. The wide range of interests manifested in our collection reflects the fact that Jamie worked in university departments of English, history and philosophy of science, and music, and that Michael was a consultant in the fields of computing, communications and automation. In 2006 we signed a deed with the National Library of Australia to ensure that our collection, which is being transferred to the Library in stages, would be preserved and made accessible to other scholars. Our choice of the National Library was motivated by its welcome interest in acquiring formed collections that would complement its existing holdings.

The items in this exhibition were created during the period that includes the end of the scientific revolution (1543–1687), the Enlightenment (1714–1830) and the start of the British colonisation of Australia, which brought to our country the English language, and its publications and ideas.

Drs Jamie and Michael Kassler

In Context

The Library

The National Library of Australia's collections are rich and ever surprising. They are also growing: as of 2022–23, the Library's physical collections ran to 273 shelf kilometres, and its digital collections totalled 2.96 petabytes. The Library is Australia's oldest national collecting institution, with origins in the Commonwealth Parliamentary Library, which served federal parliament and the nation from 1901, first in Melbourne and then in Canberra from 1927. The *National Library Act 1960* formalised the separation of the National Library and Parliamentary Library, and in August 1968, the Library opened in its current, purpose-built building.

The Library has always focused on collecting Australia's documentary heritage, and that of the Asia–Pacific region, to give context to Australia's place in the world. While in recent decades, the Library's international collecting priorities have narrowed to the Asia–Pacific region, particularly China, Indonesia, Timor-Leste and Melanesia, its rare European collections remain treasured and available to readers. It is these, as well as the Library's Australian collections, that the Kassler Collection resonates with and enhances.

For the last three years, it has been my privilege to delve into the Library's Rare Books and Music collections to 1840, to uncover their histories, quirks and secrets. The Jamie and Michael Kassler Collection, which is being donated in stages, greatly extends and deepens the Library's collections of rare prints and books, music, pictures and manuscripts from the musicological world of seventeenth-, eighteenth- and early nineteenth-century Britain. It has enormous research potential. This book samples highlights of the Kasslers' collection. The current essay explores how the Library's existing holdings intersect with it; structurally, it takes its cue from the themes you will encounter as you progress through the fascinating essays written by Drs Jamie and Michael Kassler.

The collections

Historically, the Library's collections have been developed, organised and housed by format, with many synergies and connections between them. The Kassler Collection itself includes rare and general collection books, music, manuscripts, journals, ephemera, oral histories and more.

The Library's Rare Books collections number around 158,000 items, with more in its Maps, Pictures and Asian collections. These printed collections date from the earliest years of moveable metal type in Europe (early 1450s) to the 2020s.

The Library has one of the most comprehensive collections documenting the Australian experience in print, particularly thanks to its having acquired over the years the collections of agent, librarian and collector Edward

From the National Library of Australia's Overseas Rare Books Collection

Augustus Petherick (1847–1917), bibliographer and lawyer John Alexander Ferguson (1881–1969), New Zealand-born London art dealer Rex Nan Kivell (1898–1977).

What may be less well known is that its Overseas Rare Books Collection is also very strong in the areas of the history of thought, exploration and travel, literature and the stage, history and religion. While most of these works were published in the United Kingdom, many others published in what are now France, the Netherlands and Italy are also held. Several of the Library's formed collections greatly extend its British holdings: for example, that of Scottish-born literary scholar David Nichol Smith, acquired in 1962, is particularly good on titles published in the eighteenth century, as are the country house libraries of the English Clifford and Irish De Vesci families.

The Library's Music Collection concentrates on Australian music from the 1850s onwards and feature the archives of many of the greatest names in Australian music. They include early European printed music in the formed collections of book dealer Kenneth Hince, dealer Everett Burton Helm, conductor Eugene Goossens, conductor and musicologist Richard Divall and conductor Richard Bonynge and dramatic coloratura soprano Dame Joan Sutherland. Composers represented at strength include Alfred Hill, Margaret Sutherland, Miriam Hyde, Dulcie Holland, Peter Sculthorpe, Larry Sitsky and Elena Kats-Chernin. Other major collections include the Symphony Australia Collection and the State Theatre Collection. One of the largest music collections comprises the archives of Australian powerhouse theatrical production company

J.C. Williamson Ltd (1870s–1970s), which, along with holdings in other Australian collections, were recently added to the UNESCO Australian Memory of the World Register.

The stage

The performing arts are among the Library's greatest thematic strengths, and while at their best they focus on the work of Australian performers and creators overseas and productions staged in Australia, they also stretch back to the earliest days of print in Europe. The Library's Rare Books collections feature many printed plays, particularly British, French and Italian ones. On the music side, the Music Collection features manuscript and printed scores.

Ephemera forms a significant part of the Library's holdings. Developed significantly from the 1980s, it is known as the PROMPT collection, and primarily consists of programs and tickets. These collections complement comprehensive broadsides and posters collections. The Library holds the earliest known surviving item printed in Australia—a playbill advertising an evening's entertainment at the first purpose-built theatre in Sydney, in 1796. More broadly, the Library holds extensive collections of the papers and pictorial archives of Australian composers, costume designers, directors, playwrights and performing arts companies.

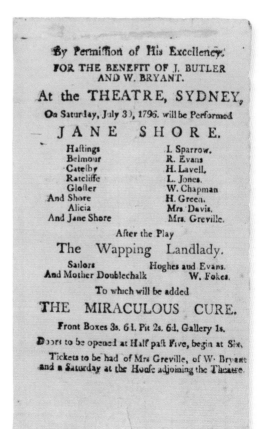

The music trade

The Kassler Collection boosts the Library's holdings of music retail history and publishing. The Library's existing collections, though they represented the world of British music publishing, were missing these scarce examples of the everyday business of music publishing and retailing.

Trade cards, bill heads and advertising flyers are extremely rare survivors that bring to life an understanding of how businesses operated centuries ago, summarising in pictorial form the key selling points of a business, its aims and its intended audience. Despite their everyday origins, they can be beautiful, and these are prime examples.

The trade cards of the Kassler Collection have counterparts in the Library's holdings of early Australian trade cards, including those engraved in Tasmania between 1825 and 1832 by the convict artist Thomas Bock (c.1790–1855), around the same time as some of these examples and an album of late nineteenth-century Victorian trade cards.

Autograph letters

The Library holds one of the largest collections of manuscripts in the country, including the papers of Australian prime ministers, governors-general, writers, academics and many more. The two manuscript letters in this book represent numerous others in the Kassler Collection. In the Library's existing collections, they complement and speak most closely to the collection of Petherick, who assembled a collection of autograph manuscript letters, including letters by John Evelyn, Richard Brinsley Sheridan, Jane Austen, Charles Dickens, George Eliot and more.

13. Queen Square Tuesday June 11.

My dear Cassandra

Your letter yesterday made me very happy.
I am heartily glad that You have escaped any share in
the Impurities of Deane, & not sorry as it turns out that
our stay here has been lengthened. — I feel tolerably secure
of our getting away next week, tho' it is certainly possible
that we may remain till Thursday the 27. — I wonder what
we shall do with all our intended visits this summer.
I should like to make a compromise with Adlestrop, Harden
& Bookham that Martha's spending the summer at
Steventon should be considered as our respective visits
to them all. — Edward has been pretty well for this last
week, & as the Waters have never disagreed with him
in any respect, we are inclined to hope that he will
derive advantage from them in the end; — every body
encourages us in this expectation, for they all say that
the effect of the Waters cannot be negative, & many
are the instances in which their benefit is felt af-
:terwards more than on the spot. — He is more com
:fortable here than I thought he would be, & so is
Eliz: — tho' they will both I believe be very glad to
get away, the latter especially. — Which one can't
wonder at somehow. — So much for Mrs Piozzi. — I had some
thoughts of writing the whole of my letter in her stile,

Giovanni Battista Piranesi (artist and etcher), *Grand'Urna di Porfido (Large Urn of Porphyry),* in *Le Antichità Romane (Roman Antiquities),* vol. 2, plate 24, Rome: Nella Stamperia Salomoni, 1784, National Library of Australia, Clifford Collection (Overseas Rare Books)

Printing

With large pictorial, cartographic and book collections, the Library's holdings represent all the major printing technologies used over the last millennium, from the printing of a Buddhist text dating from 1162, through woodcut printing, copperplate engraving, etching, mezzotint, aquatint, lithography and more, down to the digital printing of today. The Kassler Collection features beautiful examples of pictorial and musical engraving and lithography, including works in progress, laying out how the final work was created. These are particularly valuable to researchers interested in the history of printing techniques and seeking to understand the various stages of the printing process.

Education

Music education is a focus of the Kassler Collection, and it enhances the Library's other holdings which feature late nineteenth- and twentieth-century Australian music education, particularly primers for the piano. The Kassler Collection takes these holdings back in time, and gives them theoretical heft. The Library already had a later edition of James Hook's *Guida di Musica* in the Helm Collection (along with other works by Hook), but the example in this book is thought to be the first edition. John Alston's music book for the visually impaired complements existing Braille holdings, which number more than 3,000 titles.

Philosophy and theory of music

The Library's collections are rich in the history of thought more broadly, with the works of many of history's greatest thinkers represented in high numbers. These include a third edition of Sir Thomas More's *Utopia* (1518), first published in 1516, and first editions of Johannes Kepler's *Rudolphine Tables* (1627), Thomas Hobbes' *Leviathan* (1651) and Adam Smith's *The Wealth of Nations* (1776). Some of the authors featured in the Kassler Collection are represented in the Library's collections by their more well-known philosophical works. For example, the Library holds a 1654 Elzevir edition of Descartes' *Meditations* (1641).

Secrets

The books by Giambattista Della Porta and John Wilkins join existing holdings by these authors. The Kassler Collection copies offer a new dimension. The Library holds a 1597 Latin edition of Della Porta's *Natural Magic,* a much earlier edition, but one that is nowhere near as interesting to view, or as clearly used and annotated, as the Kassler Collection copy. The Library now holds seven rare editions of books by the English bishop and scientist John Wilkins, including a first edition (1641) of the title explored here.

Celebrated scores

Though it is not comprehensive, the Library's Music Collection holds many major editions of European composers, including scores published in their lifetimes.

George Frideric Handel, *Rodelinda: An Opera*, London: J. Cluer in Bow-Church-Yard, 1725, National Library of Australia, Symphony Australia Eugene Goossens Collection (Music)

For example, they include printed scores of Handel's operas *Radamisto* (1720) and *Rodelinda* (1725) and the earliest published edition of Mozart's *Requiem* (1800).

Conclusion

The Kasslers' collection of scarce—often unique—items is, in effect, a 'library within a library' of early modern to early nineteenth-century music in Britain, one that offers a wealth of detail and delight for readers interested in everything from music as a science to the music trade and its advertising. A collection originally formed by two leading scholars as a private, working music library is now available to all, for researchers of the future to use and benefit from. It is a welcome addition that sits in good company.

Dr Susannah Helman
Rare Books and Music Curator, National Library of Australia

The Stage

Broadside for a Performance of Handel's Messiah

Theatre Royal, Covent Garden

letterpress
London: Printed by E. Macleish, 21 February 1817

Each year, during the Lenten season, the Theatre Royal, Covent Garden, held a series of weekly performances of oratorios. In advance of each performance, a broadside was printed to advertise the event and attract patrons to it. The broadside featured here was printed by Elizabeth Macleish (1776–1847), who printed the majority of the theatre's playbills between 1799 and 1823.

The 21 February 1817 performance was directed by the cellist Charles Jane Ashley (1772–1843), who managed the Covent Garden Oratorios between 1816 and 1819, and featured the famous oratorio *Messiah*, composed by George Frideric Handel (1685–1759) in 1741. On that occasion, the orchestra was led by the violinist and composer William Henry Ware (1777–1828), and Samuel Wesley (1766–1837) presided at the organ.

This concert began at 7pm and lasted for several hours; patrons who arrived at 9pm paid half price. In addition to Handel's *Messiah*, the event included the first London appearance of someone described in the broadside as 'the celebrated Miss Tremean', who played a violin concerto. Contemporary newspaper accounts report that she was then about eight years old, that she was a pupil of the violinist John David Loder (1788–1846) in Bath, and that her surname was actually 'Tremearn'. Unfortunately, no record has been found of her first name.

Tickets to Concerts and Lectures

Two hundred years ago, attending concerts and lectures in London could be quite the social occasion, with no expense spared on what are usually ephemeral items. These tickets—which would have been costly to produce—were for one-off events and subscription seasons. They display the skills of English engravers, and all are based on original work by well-known painters.

1. John Thornthwaite (engraver, fl. 1771–1795); after **Mather Brown** (artist, 1761–1831), *Ticket for an Evening of 'Readings & Music' Held at Free Masons Hall, London*, 1790–1817, engraving

2. Abraham Raimbach (engraver, 1776–1843); after **Richard Westall** (artist, 1765–1836), *Ticket for the Royal Institution, London*, 1799–1805, engraving

The ticket depicts Minerva (Roman goddess of wisdom) and the nine muses (Greek goddesses of literature, science and the arts). It also includes a somewhat truncated quote from Cicero: *Omnes artes habent quoddam commune vinculum* ('All arts have some common bond').

The Royal Institution, founded in 1799, offered many courses of lectures, which were attended by women as well as by men. Initially, these dealt with natural and experimental philosophy and its application to the mechanical arts, but financial problems prompted the proprietors to branch out to more popular subjects. In 1805, the composer William Crotch (1775–1847) was engaged to give six lectures on music, and he and others delivered similar lectures in subsequent years. The lectures were educationally important: until University College, London, was founded in 1826, the city had no university, and Oxford and Cambridge were available only to men. The Royal Institution acted as a model for later examples: London Institution (1806), Surrey Institution (1807) and Russell Institution (1808).

3. James Mitan (engraver, 1776–1822); after **Richard Cosway** (artist, 1742–1821), *Ticket for New Musical Fund, Established 1786*, 1812–17, etching and engraving

4. Richard Sawyer (1785–1852), *Ticket for New Musical Fund, Subscribers Ticket* 10 April 1828, engraving

The New Musical Fund was a charity established in 1786 to provide relief to infirm musicians, their widows and their children. Its income came from subscribers and from the sale of tickets to its benefit concerts held annually in London.

The Mitan engraving featured on tickets to the charity's benefit concerts at least between 1812 and 1817; the Sawyer one was printed for performance at the King's Theatre, Haymarket, on 10 April 1828, conducted by Sir George Smart (1776–1867).

5. Joseph Skelton (engraver, 1783–1871); after **Giovanni Battista Cipriani** (artist, 1727–1785), *Ticket for Theatre, Oxford: 1st Concert*, 2 June 1818, engraving

This ticket, printed for a performance of Handel's oratorio *Messiah* at the Theatre in Oxford on the 2 June 1818, features Apollo, the god of music. The concert was held on the first day of a three-day Oxford Grand Musical Festival.

1.

2.

3.

4.

5.

John Gay (1685–1732)

The Beggar's Opera: As It Is Acted at the Theatre-Royal in Lincolns-Inn-Fields

London: Printed for John Watts, 2nd ed., 1728

The poet and dramatist John Gay is principally remembered for having written the words of *The Beggar's Opera*, which opened in London on 29 January 1728. The character Peachum was seen to ridicule Sir Robert Walpole, British prime minister from 1721 to 1742, and that of Polly to satirise his mistress (and later wife), Maria Skerritt. The opera offended Walpole, who banned Gay's 1729 sequel, *Polly*, from the theatres, although it, like *The Beggar's Opera*, was published and widely sold in multiple editions.

The Beggar's Opera is considered to be the first ballad opera, defined as a work in which actors and actresses sing short songs between their spoken dialogues. It began with a musical overture composed by John Christopher Pepusch (1667–1752). The opera ran for 62 nights during its first season and received numerous subsequent performances in London and elsewhere.

The opera's influence continued into the twentieth century, when a German translation of its text by Elisabeth Hauptmann led to her collaborating with the playwright Bertolt Brecht and the composer Kurt Weill to create *Die Dreigroschenoper*. Its indebtedness to *The Beggar's Opera* was acknowledged in the playbill of its first performance in Berlin in 1928. The Brecht–Weill work has been well known in the English-speaking world as *The Threepenny Opera* from the 1930s and continues to be performed in many countries.

THE
BEGGAR's
OPERA.

As it is Acted at the

THEATRE-ROYAL

IN

LINCOLNS-INN-FIELDS.

Written by Mr. *GAY*.

———*Nos hæc novimus effe nihil.*   Mart.

The SECOND EDITION:

To which is Added

The OUVERTURE in SCORE;
And the MUSICK *prefix'd to each* SONG.

LONDON:
Printed for JOHN WATTS, at the Printing-Office
in *Wild-Court*, near *Lincoln's-Inn-Fields*.
MDCCXXVIII.
[Price 1s. 6d.]

Joseph Haydn (1732–1809)

The Creation: A Sacred Oratorio

Worcester: Printed and sold by J. Tymbs, 1803

The Austrian composer Franz Joseph Haydn lived in London from 1791 to 1792, and again from 1794 to 1795. Known as the father of both the symphony and the string quartet, Haydn was a friend and mentor to Wolfgang Amadeus Mozart and taught Ludwig van Beethoven. His oratorio *Die Schöpfung (The Creation)*, composed to a libretto by Gottfried van Swieten (1733–1803), received its first performance in Vienna in 1799 and was first published there in 1800, with text in both German and English. At Haydn's request, the music historian Charles Burney (1726–1814) solicited numerous English subscribers to its publication. The work received its first English performances in London and elsewhere that year. It continues to be regularly performed today in many countries.

The pamphlet featured here contains the oratorio's English text, issued to accompany its performance in Worcester on 28 September 1803. This particular pamphlet is a reprint of the one Tymbs had published for the work's first Worcester performance three years earlier. Pamphlets such as this are quite rare, as they would have been discarded after the performance.

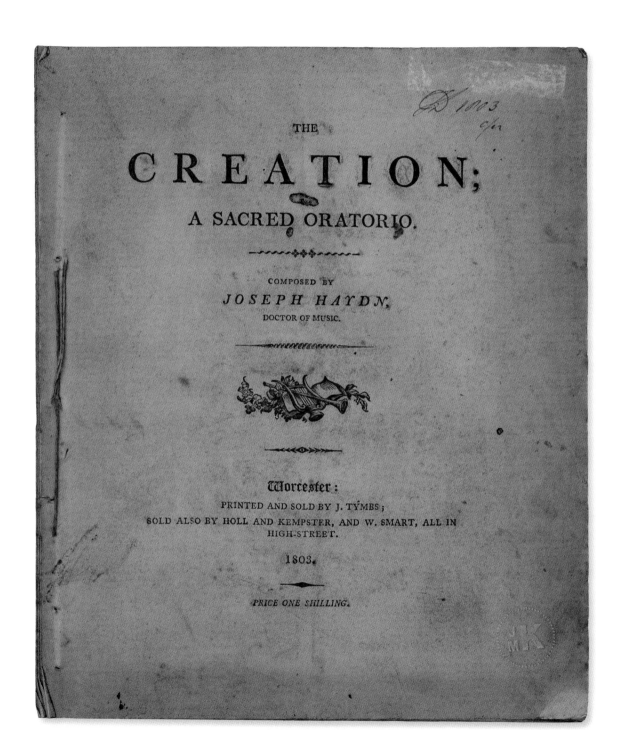

THE

CREATION;

A SACRED ORATORIO.

COMPOSED BY

JOSEPH HAYDN,

DOCTOR OF MUSIC.

Worcester:

PRINTED AND SOLD BY J. TYMBS;
SOLD ALSO BY HOLL AND KEMPSTER, AND W. SMART, ALL IN
HIGH-STREET.

1803.

PRICE ONE SHILLING.

Joseph Constantine Stadler (watercolourist, c.1755–1828)
Augustus Charles Pugin (engraver, 1762–1832)
after Thomas Rowlandson (artist, 1757–1827)

The Surrey Institution Lecture Hall

aquatint and hand-coloured engraving
London: R. Ackermann, 1 September 1809

The Surrey Institution, London, was founded by subscribers in 1807 to promote scientific, literary and musical education and research. It renovated the Rotunda Building in what was then the County of Surrey (hence the institution's name) to include a lecture hall that accommodated 500 people. The hall opened to audiences in 1808. Lecture courses on music, often supplemented by performances of the music being studied, were given there by Samuel Wesley between 1809 and 1811 and by William Crotch between 1812 and 1823. Crotch's annotated syllabus of his 1813 course of lectures is also featured in this publication (see pages 30–31).

The hall, a lecturer and an audience of men and women are delineated in this work by Joseph Constantine Stadler. Published individually by the London book and print seller Rudolph Ackermann (1764–1834), it was reprinted in volume 3 of his *The Microcosm of London* (c.1809).

Stadler was born in Germany but was active in London between 1780 and 1812. Augustus Charles Pugin was born in France and worked in London after the French Revolution as an artist and architectural draughtsman. Thomas Rowlandson was a well-known English artist and caricaturist.

SURREY INSTITUTION.

London Pub. Sept.r 1.st 1809, at R.Ackermann's Repository of Arts 101 Strand.

The Music Trade

Music Seller Advertisements

The British and Irish music trades in the eighteenth and nineteenth centuries were based upon shopkeepers called 'music sellers' who sold printed music and instruments on which it could be played. These sellers often issued printed trade cards and invoices to let customers know their location and their wares. Five such items are shown here.

1. George Burder (artist and engraver, 1752–1832), *Trade Card for London Music Sellers Longman & Co.*, 1773–77, engraving

Longman & Co. had a shop at No. 26 Cheapside, where they hung a sign featuring Apollo, the Greek god of music. George Burder began business as a London engraver about 1773, and in his memoir he recorded being 'much engaged in musical pursuits' in 1773, which could have led to his connection with Longman & Co. He appears to have started preaching in 1776 and to have stopped engraving soon afterwards.

1.

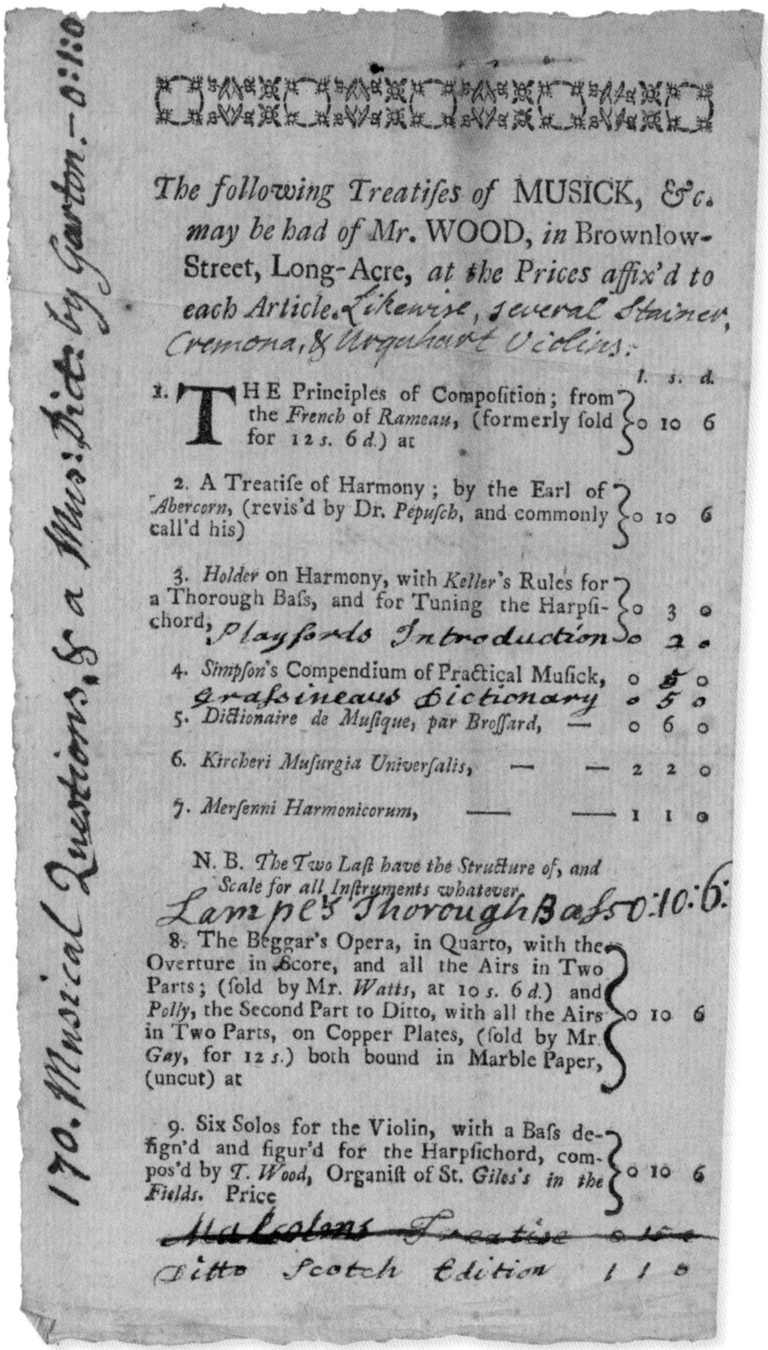

170. Musical Questions, & a Mus: Dict: by Garton. – 0:1:0

The following Treatifes of MUSICK, *&c. may be had of Mr.* WOOD, *in* Brownlow-Street, Long-Acre, *at the Prices affix'd to each Article.* Likewise, several Stainer, Cremona, & Urquhart Violins:

	l.	s.	d.
1. THE Principles of Compofition; from the *French* of *Rameau*, (formerly fold for 12 *s.* 6 *d.*) at	0	10	6
2. A Treatife of Harmony; by the Earl of *Abercorn*, (revis'd by Dr. *Pepufch*, and commonly call'd his)	0	10	6
3. *Holder* on Harmony, with *Keller*'s Rules for a Thorough Bafs, and for Tuning the Harpfichord,	0	3	0
Playfords Introduction	0	2	0
4. *Simpfon*'s Compendium of Practical Mufick,	0	5	0
Grassineaus Dictionary	0	5	0
5. *Dictionaire de Mufique, par Broffard,* —	0	6	0
6. *Kircheri Mufurgia Univerfalis,* — —	2	2	0
7. *Merfenni Harmonicorum,* — —	1	1	0

N. B. *The Two Laft have the Structure of, and Scale for all Inftruments whatever.*

	l.	s.	d.
Lampe's Thorough Bass	0	10	6
8. The Beggar's Opera, in Quarto, with the Overture in Score, and all the Airs in Two Parts; (fold by Mr. *Watts*, at 10 *s.* 6 *d.*) and *Polly*, the Second Part to Ditto, with all the Airs in Two Parts, on Copper Plates, (fold by Mr. *Gay*, for 12 *s.*) both bound in Marble Paper, (uncut) at	0	10	6
9. Six Solos for the Violin, with a Bafs defign'd and figur'd for the Harpfichord, compos'd by *T. Wood*, Organift of St. *Giles's in the Fields.* Price	0	10	6
~~Malcolms Treatise~~	~~0~~	~~1~~	~~0~~
Ditto Scotch Edition	1	1	0

2.

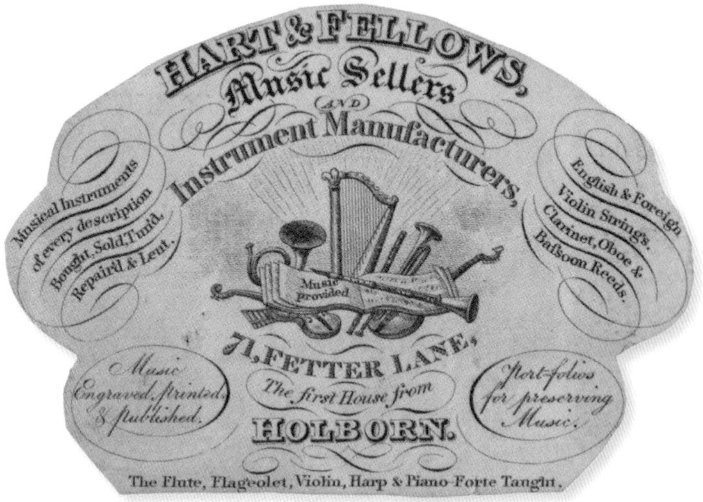

3.

2. ***Annotated Advertising Flyer for London Bookseller Thomas Wood***, c.1783, letterpress and iron gall ink

The flyer is headed 'The following treatises of musick, &c. may be had of Mr. Wood, in Brownlow-Street, Long-Acre'. Wood is identifiable as the London bookseller Thomas Wood (d.1783) because the February 1784 sale catalogue of the 'collection of books ... the property of Mr Thomas Wood, deceased ... on the premises, Brownlow-Street, Long-Acre' includes several music treatises listed in this advertisement. No other copy of this item has been found. (This item, in common with other early advertisements, was printed on normal-weight paper rather than on a thicker card.)

3. ***Trade Card or Letterhead for Hart & Fellows, Music Sellers and Instrument Manufacturers, 71 Fetter Lane, near Holborn,*** 1818–26, engraving

This firm, a partnership between Joseph Hart (c.1797–1856) and George Fellows (dates unknown), appears to have been located in Fetter Lane between 1818 and 1826. The firm was dissolved on 7 February 1828. No other copy of this item has been found.

4. **Jonas Radford** (engraver, active 1826–42) and
S.Y. Griffith & Co. (printers, active 1820–30),
*Trade Card for Cooper, Musical Instrument &
Music Seller, 406 High Street, Cheltenham,*
c.1826, engraving

Samuel Young Griffith was active c.1820–30, and
this card was printed on an unnumbered page
in his book *Griffith's New Historical Description
of Cheltenham ... Embellished with Copperplate
Engravings*, 2nd ed., vol. 1 (London: Longman,
Rees, Orme, Brown & Green, 1826). In that volume,
'Cooper's Harp and Piano-Forte Warehouse, and
Circulating Library of Music' is described and its
proprietor, Mrs Cooper, is identified as 'a professor
of the harp and piano-forte'. She was active as a music
teacher and music seller in Cheltenham between
1812 and 1826.

5. *Trade Card for S.J. Pigott's Dublin Shop,
The Dublin Harmonic Institution,
112 Grafton Street*, 1836–53, engraving

The Dublin Harmonic Institution, an Irish music
seller and publisher, moved to its 112 Grafton Street
address in December 1836, when Samuel James
Pigott (1797–1853) was its proprietor. The only
other known copy of this card has been pasted onto
a volume of Beethoven string quartets published
in 1846.

4.

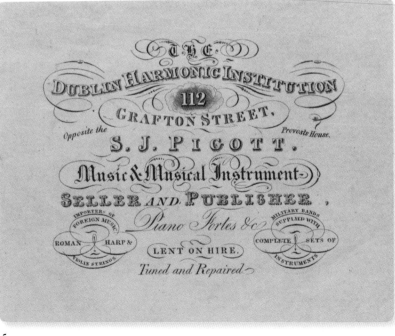

5.

Autograph
Letters

Number of Lecture_ the Terms six Guineas per ture.

*I am
Dear Sir,
respectfully yours
Wesley*

William Herschel (1738–1822)

Letter to Tiberius Cavallo

handwritten letter and wax seal, 8 December 1788

William Herschel was a musician and astronomer best known for his discovery of the planet Uranus in 1781. He was born in Hannover, Germany, but moved to England in 1757, where he held various musical positions and sought to make a name for himself as a composer. He went on to make further astronomical discoveries working with his sister Caroline, whom he introduced to the study of astronomy. Herschel was made a knight of the Royal Guelphic Order of Hannover in 1816. He helped found the Astronomical Society of London (later the Royal Astronomical Society) in 1820, and was its first president.

In this letter, he informs Tiberius Cavallo (1749–1809), an Italian natural philosopher and writer on musical temperament, that 'a lady has taken a liking to' Herschel's piano forte in his home in Slough, Buckinghamshire, and 'wishes to have such a one'. He asks Cavallo to 'do me the favour to procure one' and 'when it can be sent I will furnish you with a direction where it is to go'. The price Herschel had mentioned to this lady was 20 guineas (£21). Herschel goes on to ask Cavallo, who lived in London, 'What news in the philosophical world?' Herschel and Cavallo were both Fellows of the Royal Society.

In a subsequent letter dated 15 December 1788, now in the Edinburgh University Library, Herschel advises Cavallo that the piano forte is to be sent to Mrs Constantia Langton in Hitcham, Suffolk, whose mother-in-law was the sister of John Pitt, the first husband of Herschel's wife, Mary née Baldwin (1750–1832).

Cavallo's involvement in securing a piano may be related to the circumstance that he was a customer of the harpsichord and piano forte manufacturer John Broadwood (1732–1812), who sought his advice regarding the best place for hammers to strike piano strings. ⟶

Dear Sir

A Lady has taken a liking
to my Piano forte and wishes to have
such a one as soon as convenient.
Will you do me the favour to pro
cure one, and when it can be
sent I will furnish you with
a direction where it is to go.
The price I have mentioned is
20 Guineas. What news in the
philosophical world? Adieu
                    Yours faithfully
                    Wm Herschel

Slough
Decr 8. 1788.

Samuel Wesley (1766–1837)

Letter to William Haseldine Pepys

handwritten letter, 23 November 1827

The composer and organist Samuel Wesley was the son of Charles Wesley (1707–1788) and the nephew of John Wesley (1703–1791), the two founders of Methodism. Charles was a prolific author of hymns, writing more than 6,500 in his lifetime.

Samuel Wesley was an active promoter of the music of Johann Sebastian Bach (1685–1750), and prepared, with the German-born musician Charles Frederick Horn (1762–1830), an influential English edition of Bach's '48' (*The Well-Tempered Clavier*, Books 1 and 2) that was published in London in four volumes between 1810 and 1813.

In his 23 November 1827 letter to William Haseldine Pepys (1775–1856), secretary of the London Institution, Wesley writes: 'I feel no Objection to repeat a Course of Lectures similar to that delivered at the Royal Institution last season ... The Number of Lectures was Eight and the Terms Six Guineas per Lecture'. The lectures were accompanied by performances of musical examples.

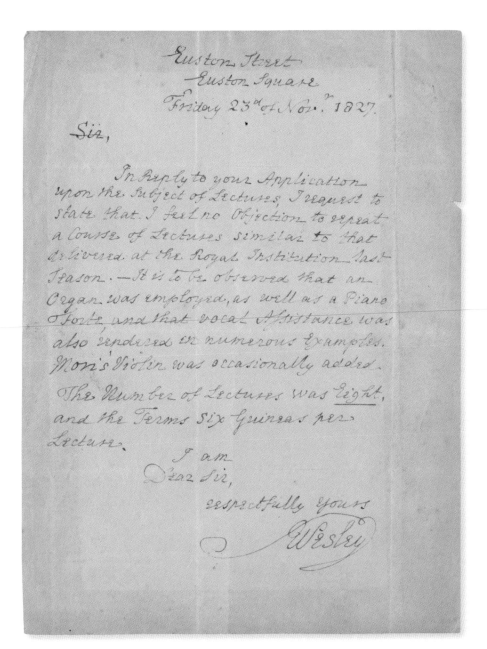

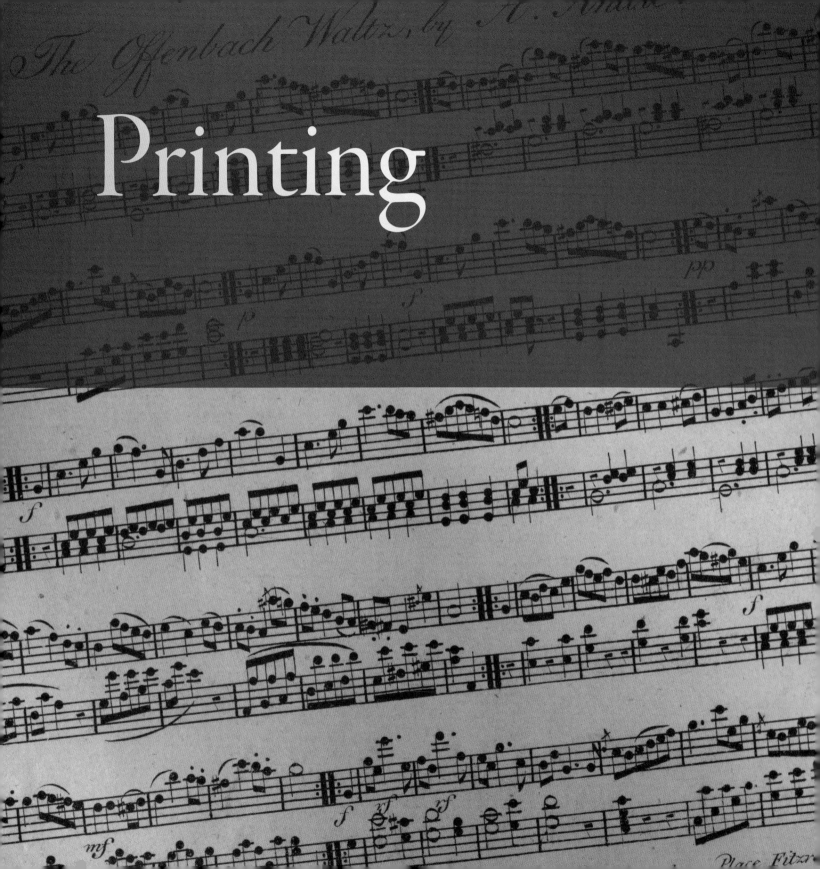

Printing

George Bickham the Elder (1684–1758)

Musick

engraving, c.1738

This page was engraved by George Bickham and was printed as plate no. 65 and item no. XXIII in his book *The Universal Penman*, published in London in instalments between 1733 and 1741 and subsequently reprinted. The most ambitious writing book of the eighteenth century, this compilation of more than 200 calligraphic specimens covered a variety of topics, including this one dealing with music.

Bickham's drawing of musicians heads the page, followed by calligraphic lettering produced by W. Clark.

Two quotations about music are included. The first is taken from Nicholas Ling's collection of prose quotations titled *Politeuphuia, or Wits Commonwealth* (1688): 'Musick is an insearchable and excellent Art, which rejoiceth the Spirits and unloadeth Grief from the heart, and consisteth in time and number.'

The second comes from William Congreve's *A Hymn to Harmony: Written in Honour of St Cecilia's Day, MDCCI* (1702): 'Musick alone with sudden Charms can bind The wand'ring Sense, & calm the troubled Mind.'

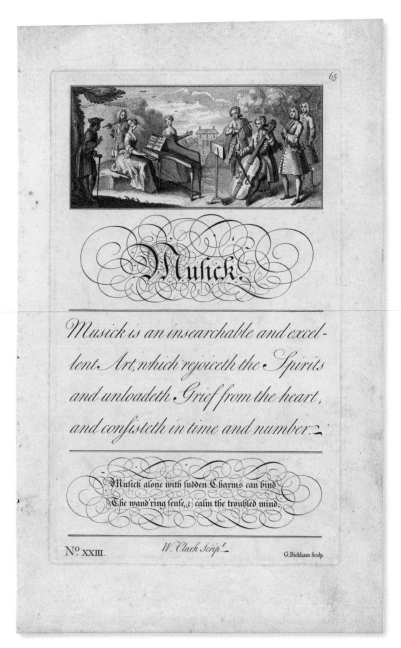

Mary Ann Rigg (engraver, 1754–1799)
after Thomas Gainsborough (artist, 1727–1788)

John Stanley

proof of stipple engraving, 1781

This half-length portrait in oval of the blind organist, violinist and composer John Stanley (1712–1786) was engraved by Mary Ann Rigg after a now lost painting by Thomas Gainsborough. She published the engraving in London on 9 April 1781 and advertised it for sale a few days later, so this proof, of which no other copy is known, must have been made shortly before then. Before later copies of the engraving were printed, some additional letters were engraved below the portrait. Dark dotted marks on the proof show where these were to be inserted. Following Rigg's marriage to the engraver Edmund Scott (1758–1815) in October 1781, the engraving's lettering was further altered to change her name to 'Scott' and to list her husband and 'Mrs Ryland' as its sellers.

Stanley had been blinded in an accident at the age of two and began to study music five years later. In 1723, he received his first of several appointments as an organist. Six years later, he became the youngest person to graduate from the University of Oxford with a Bachelor of Music degree. He was elected organist to the Society of the Inner Temple in 1734, and became a governor of the Foundling Hospital in 1770, where he was active in its musical affairs. In 1779, Stanley was appointed Master of the King's Band of Musicians.

From about 1758, the hospital gave blind children instruction in music, using an apparatus whose details are not known. By 1770, Stanley learned that Thomas Grenville (c.1746–1827), also a blind organist, had invented an apparatus for teaching blind children the rules of arithmetic. He made this known to the Society of Arts in a letter jointly written with the philanthropist Jonas Hanway (1712–1786), who had helped reform the hospital. Grenville's invention was deposited in the society's repository, and he was awarded a bounty of 15 guineas. After Stanley's death, two inventions for teaching music to the blind were listed by the society, but such aids had never been available to Stanley, who had to rely on his own resources, including a sensitivity to touch, an excellent memory and 'a musical ear'.

Johann Anton André (1775–1842)

The Offenbach Waltz

lithograph
London: Printed and sold by G.J. Vollweiler at his polyautographic office, c.1807

The Offenbach Waltz is a rare example of early English lithographed music. No other copies of this publication are known to exist. At this time, music was commonly printed from engraved plates; music type was used occasionally.

Lithographic printing was invented by Alois Senefelder (1771–1834) in Munich about 1798. In 1779, he and his partner signed a contract with Johann Anton André, head of his family's music-publishing business in Offenbach-am-Main (near Frankfurt, Germany), which enabled the firm to make use of Senefelder's method of chemical printing. André explored opportunities to use the technology in several European countries, and sent Senefelder to London to secure English and Scottish patents for it. These were granted, and sold to André in 1801.

André then arranged for his brother Philippe André to establish an enterprise in London to exploit the new printing process, and a lithographic press was installed there. In contrast to the André firm, which used lithography to print music in Offenbach, Philippe devoted his efforts to publishing reproductions of artists' drawings, beginning in 1803 with a series called *Specimens of Polyautography*. (The term 'polyautography' reflected lithography's ability to produce multiple copies of handwriting; the English word 'lithography' was not used until 1813.)

Philippe left London in 1804 and was succeeded there at the end of 1805 by Georg Jacob Vollweiler (1770–1847), who had taught music to Johann Anton André in 1792–93 and who later worked for his firm and lived in his home in Offenbach. In 1806–07, at his 'polyautographic office' in London, Vollweiler published, in addition to artists' drawings, 12 music compositions, including *The Offenbach Waltz*. However, the London business did not succeed, and Vollweiler returned to Offenbach in 1807.

The music of *The Offenbach Waltz* is a shortened version of *Walze favorite du carnaval d'Offenbach* that the firm had published in 1802. Presumably, Vollweiler decided to re-lithograph the reduced version in London in homage to his employer and former pupil.

While Johann Anton André's music is now forgotten, he is remembered for his lithographic efforts and for purchasing hundreds of Mozart manuscripts from the composer's widow in 1799, and for directing his firm to catalogue and publish much of Mozart's music.

Also shown above is a souvenir box produced about 2005 by Musikhaus André, Offenbach-am-Main, to illustrate early lithographic music printing, which this firm pioneered in 1800. The process, which in its early days required notation to be drawn in reverse on stone, is exemplified in the box by an extract from Mozart's *Eine kleine Nachtmusik*.

Education

Robert Bremner (c.1713–1789)

The Rudiments of Music: Or, a Short and Easy Treatise on That Subject

London: Printed for the author, 3rd ed., 1763

In 1754, Robert Bremner opened a shop in Edinburgh where he sold music, musical instruments and books about music. In 1762, he moved to London, where business opportunities were much greater, and opened a second music shop there, leaving the Edinburgh business in the care of a manager.

Bremner had been a pupil of the Italian violinist, composer and music theorist Francesco Geminiani (1687–1762), perhaps in Dublin, as Geminiani is not known to have visited Scotland. They appear to have been in contact in 1760, when Bremner 'printed for the author' Geminiani's *The Art of Playing the Guitar or Cittra*.

The Rudiments of Music was published in three editions, the first two in Edinburgh in 1756 and 1762, and the third 'with considerable additions' in London. The first and second editions were dedicated to the Lord Provost of Edinburgh, to other notables of that city and to the 'Honourable and Reverend Members of the Committee for improving Church-music' that was appointed in 1756. This committee's first task was to select 'a proper number' of the best tunes to be sung in churches. Bremner was authorised to publish these tunes, which he did both separately and as an annex to this book. He pointed out that almost all worshippers could read words, but few could read music and thus lacked the ability to sing unfamiliar tunes. Bremner, therefore, decried 'the power of every organist or church-clerk to introduce what tunes he pleases' and suggested that 'a select number of psalm-tunes should be appointed by the Legislature for the established Churches in Great Britain'.

In contrast to existing treatises written for 'those who make music their profession, or who chuse [*sic*] it for a science which they incline to study in its full extent', in this book Bremner's aim was 'to make the first principles of this science so plain and intelligible, that any attentive reader of ordinary capacity may understand as much of the theory as is necessary for practice'. Accordingly, his treatise describes scales, staves, notes and rests, clefs, bars, tones and semitones, sharps and flats, keynotes and other fundamentals of music notation.

This book bears the bookplate of the potter Josiah Wedgwood (1730–1795). However, the handwritten annotations to its text were not written by him. ⟶

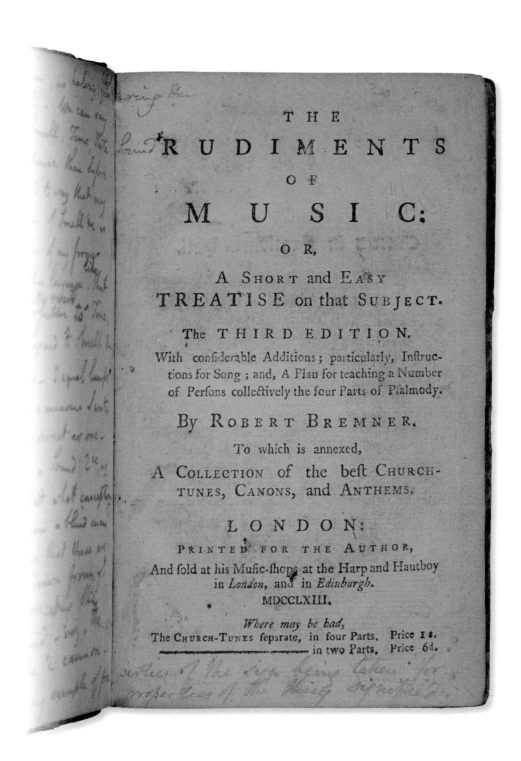

THE
RUDIMENTS
OF
MUSIC:
OR,

A SHORT and EASY
TREATISE on that SUBJECT.

The THIRD EDITION.

With considerable Additions; particularly, Instructions for Song; and, A Plan for teaching a Number
of Persons collectively the four Parts of Psalmody.

By ROBERT BREMNER.

To which is annexed,

A COLLECTION of the best CHURCH-
TUNES, CANONS, and ANTHEMS.

LONDON:

PRINTED FOR THE AUTHOR,

And sold at his Music-shops at the Harp and Hautboy
in *London*, and in *Edinburgh*.
MDCCLXIII.

Where may be had,
The CHURCH-TUNES separate, in four Parts. Price 1 s.
———————————— in two Parts. Price 6 d.

James Hook (1746–1827)

Guida di Musica: Being a Complete Book of Instructions for Beginners on the Harpsichord or Piano Forte

London: Printed and sold by J[ohn] Preston, [1785]

James Hook, the organist at London's Vauxhall Gardens from 1773 to 1820, was a prolific composer who wrote more than 2,000 songs. Something of a child prodigy, he played instruments from the age of four, performing in public from the age of six. He also taught many pupils to play a variety of keyboard instruments.

Hook designed *Guida di Musica (Music Guide)*, whose first edition is shown here, 'on a new plan, calculated to save a great deal of time & trouble both to Master & Scholar'. The work, written for use by beginners, sets out to teach them the names of the notes of the C major scale and shows their placement and fingering on treble and bass staves, and introduces them to flats, sharps, naturals, different note lengths, and so on. Following the initial instructions, the book includes 24 'progressive-lessons in various keys, with the fingering marked throughout'.

The popularity of *Guida di Musica* is indicated by its reissue in several editions and by novelist Jane Austen's reference to 'Hook's Lessons for beginners' in an 1813 letter to her sister, Cassandra.

Anton Bemetzrieder (1739–1817)
Daniel Orme (engraver, 1766–1837)

Announcement of 'Bemetzrieder's Musical Academy for the Principles and Solfaing',
with Handwritten Message to Ludwig ['Louis'] Count Starhemberg

etching, engraving and ink, c.1796

The musician Anton Bemetzrieder was born in France and obtained degrees in philosophy and law from the University of Strasbourg. In 1769, he met the philosopher Denis Diderot, whose daughter became his pupil. Two years later, he published his first book on music, *Leçons de clavecin, et principes d'harmonie*, which Diderot edited. A poor English translation of this book was published in London in 1778–79 under the title *Music Made Easy to Every Capacity*. In 1781, Bemetzrieder moved to London, where he re-edited, expanded and translated his earlier instruction books on music. In addition to teaching and composing music, he wrote books on philosophy.

The announcement of his London academy was printed about 1796 from two engraved plates. The top plate has a 1796 etching and engraving by Daniel Orme, who lived in London from 1785 to 1814 and became historical engraver to King George III and the Prince of Wales (the future King George IV). This engraving has at the centre a half-length portrait of Bemetzrieder in an oval, surrounded on the left by Apollo (the Greek god of music) with his lyre, and on the right by a woman with books

and instruments (representing philosophy). The engraved word 'Bemetzrieder's' on the top plate refers to the content of the bottom plate, which gives information about his academy. The Kassler Collection includes a complete copy of the announcement printed from both plates.

The item shown here is a separate sheet of paper printed from just the top plate of the announcement, which includes Bemetzrieder's handwritten message to Ludwig (known as Louis in England) Count Starhemberg (1762–1833), Austrian ambassador to Britain. Starhemberg subscribed to Bemetzrieder's *Musical Poem for Voice and Piano-forte or Harp*, which was published in parts from April 1804. In this message, Bemetzrieder notes that Starhemberg had 'paid half a Guinea on his subscription; and may hear the work at his own house'.

Bemetzrieder used paper printed from just the top plate to write at least one other message: a note, dated 1 November 1804, to the music historian Charles Burney (1726–1814), requesting a time when Burney could hear a performance of the *Musical Poem*, is in the British Museum.

William Crotch (1775–1847)

Annotated Fragment of Syllabus of a Course of Lectures on Music to Be Delivered at the Surry [sic] *Institution*

letterpress and ink

London: [likely printed by Schulze and Dean], 1813

Between 1812 and 1823 the composer William Crotch, who had been elected Heather Professor of Music at Oxford in 1797, aged 21, gave various courses of lectures on music at the Surrey Institution in London. Crotch has been described as 'a child prodigy without parallel in the history of music', who is known to have performed from the age of two. Syllabuses for these courses were printed and distributed to inform potential attendees of the topics to be covered.

Crotch has annotated this syllabus for his 1813 lectures, listing the dates when he delivered each of the eight lectures, beginning on 29 January. He was a prolific lecturer. Besides those he delivered at the Surrey Institution and the University of Oxford, he also gave courses of lectures on music in the Royal Institution, London.

Copies of Crotch's Surrey Institution syllabuses are rare. No other copies of this particular one have ever been located, nor of the 1815 and 1816 syllabuses that are also in the Kassler Collection. Copies of the 1817, 1819 and 1821 syllabuses are in Sir John Soane's Museum, London, and a copy of the 1823 syllabus is in the British Library.

To commence on *Friday the* 29th *of January* 1813, *at* 7 o'Clock *in the Evening* precisely.

Friday 29. LECTURE I. Music of the Antients. National Music of the German and Spanish Jews, and of the Highland and Lowland Scotch.

F. Feb. 5. LECTURE II. National Music of the British and Welsh, together with other Music of uncertain origin. National Music of France, Italy, Switzerland, Germany, Spain, Portugal, Hungary, Poland, Scandinavia, Norway, Denmark, Russia, Turkey, Sclavonia, Persia, China, the East Indies, Otaheite and America.

F. — 9. LECTURE III. Scientific Music in the early part of the Eighteenth Century. Croft, Steffani, Leo, and Pergolesi.

F. — 12. LECTURE IV. Middle of the Eighteenth Century. Comparison between the Operas of the Germans and Italians. Terradellas, Hasse, Vinci. Concert Music. Geminiani and Ricciotti.

F. — 16. LECTURE V. Latter part of the Eighteenth Century. Oratorios and Operas of Jomelli. Sonatas of Charles Philip Emanuel Bach. Operas and other Music of John Christian Bach.

F. — 19. LECTURE VI. Chamber Music of the same period. Sonatas of Vanhall. Remarks on the Difference of Character in the various Keys. Schobert, Boccherini, and Kozeluch.

F. — 23. LECTURE VII. The Quartetts of Pleyel; the Harp Music of Krumpholtz; and the Piano-Forte Sonatas of Hüllmandell and Clementi.

F. — 26. LECTURE VIII. The Vocal Music of Mozart.

Charles Wheatstone (1802–1875)

The Harmonic Diagram Invented by C. Wheatstone

engraving

London: C. Wheatstone, 1824

Charles Wheatstone is remembered principally for his inventions and publications in acoustics, telegraphy, electricity and optics. In 1834, he was appointed professor of experimental philosophy at King's College, London, in recognition of his achievements in those areas. He was knighted in 1868.

Wheatstone was born into a family of musicians and music sellers who intended him to follow such a career path. At the age of 14, he was apprenticed to his uncle, a London music seller (also named Charles Wheatstone). When his uncle died in 1823, Wheatstone and his brother William took over the business. Their March 1824 advertisement in the periodical *The Harmonicon* listed more than 40 music compositions 'recently published by C. Wheatstone'. It also listed, under the heading 'Musical Theory', 'C. Wheatstone's Harmonic Diagram' for sale at four shillings.

The diagram consists of a printed card to which a rotatable disc has been attached. A small aperture on the disc is normally blocked from view, but when this is opened by a ribbon the text printed behind it is revealed. The diagram can be used to select a keynote and find the notes of its major and minor keys. It can also facilitate transposition from one key to another.

In a pamphlet accompanying the diagram, Wheatstone acknowledged that it was not a substitute for existing theoretical treatises, but could assist pupils to gain a rudimentary knowledge of musical scales.

John Alston (1778–1846)

Musical Catechism, with Tunes, for the Use of the Blind

Glasgow: Printed in the Asylum, by the Institution Press, 1838

John Alston was a Glasgow muslin manufacturer and town councillor who served as Honorary Treasurer of the Asylum for the Blind in the city from 1825. He spent a good deal of time with its students, and in the 1830s, he developed a system to typeset books for the blind that used embossed capital letters of the English alphabet, shaped in such a way that users could distinguish them by touch. Much experimentation was involved in this work, which culminated in the printing of the whole Bible in December 1840. Fourteen thousand copies of this Bible had been printed in the asylum by 1844, for use by families or institutions. Until Braille later supplanted it, 'Alston type' was the principal method of printing books for the blind in Britain.

The education of the blind at the asylum included musical literacy, and to produce his *Musical Catechism*, Alston devised type that printed embossed music symbols such as notes and rests. The work poses various elementary questions, such as 'What is harmony?', and gives answers to them. The music portion of the work consists of the sort of simple tunes traditionally sung in Scottish religious worship.

This book was published in at least three editions but is now quite rare.

MUSICAL CATECHISM,

WITH TUNES,

FOR THE USE OF THE BLIND.

GLASGOW:
PRINTED IN THE ASYLUM, BY THE INSTITUTION PRESS.
1838.
PRICE THREE SHILLINGS AND SIXPENCE.

A Philosophy and Theory of Music

A NEW THEORY OF MUSICAL HARMONY,

ACCORDING TO A COMPLETE AND NATURAL

SYSTEM OF THAT SCIENCE.

BY

AUGUSTUS FREDERICK CHRISTOPHER KOLLMANN,

ORGANIST OF HIS MAJESTY'S GERMAN CHAPEL AT ST. JAMES'S.

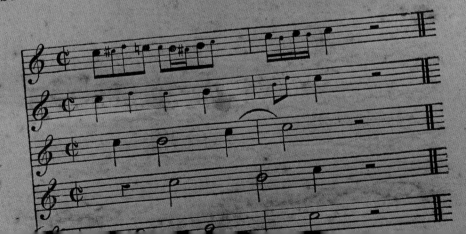

Charles Butler (1571–1647)

The Principles of Musik, in Singing and Setting: with the Two-fold Use Thereof [Ecclesiasticall and Civil]

London: Printed by John Haviland, for the author, 1636

The English priest, philologist, apiarist and amateur musician Charles Butler entered Magdalen College, Oxford, in 1579, graduating Bachelor of Arts in 1584 and Master of Arts in 1587. At Oxford, he served as a Bible clerk, and from 1579 to 1585 as a chorister. After leaving Oxford in 1593, he served as parish rector in a church near Basingstoke, then in 1595 as Master of the Holy Ghost School in Basingstoke and in 1600 as vicar of Wootton St Lawrence, where he remained until his death. Little else is known about his life except that he published several books, including those on grammar, rhetoric and oratory—the last suggesting that the Holy Ghost School was a grammar school where he taught Latin and probably music.

Butler's last publication was *The Principles of Musik,* dedicated to King Charles I. The work was divided into two 'Books'. The longer Book I presents what he called the 'essence' of the art; that is, its 'systems of rules and precepts'. It is an instruction manual proceeding through the fundamentals of music, sight singing, simple composition and then more complex composition. Butler drew upon two ancient music systems: the hexachord system as the unit of scale analysis, and the five modes (Dorian, Lydian, Aeolian, Phrygian and Ionian) as the unit for sets of scales purported to have ethical properties.

Book II, a discourse on the use of music, ecclesiastical and civil, has two parts. The first part discusses music in the service of God, drawing on Old and New Testament texts, on early commentaries on those texts by St Augustine and others, and on what emerged from various ecumenical councils. The second part deals with music as the care and comfort of mankind. In addition to biblical texts, Butler refers here to a range of secular authors, including philosophers such as Aristotle, Boethius and Plato, and poets such as Homer.

In several places in *The Principles of Musik*, Butler replies to various objections while not naming their sources. These objections include: (1) that 'exquisite' music hinders the service of God; (2) that the true worship of God does not consist in outward graces and ornaments; (3) that 'artificial' music cannot be had in all churches; and (4) that civil music is but vanity which does more harm than good. These objections suggest that their source was Puritan dissenters who disliked the elaborate ceremonies of the Catholic and Anglican churches, including the use of organs, which were banned for 10 years from 7 May 1644.

Before 163,3 Butler attempted to standardise orthography by developing a system that used letters in the Anglo-Saxon and Latin alphabets and symbols perhaps of his own invention. For example, he represented the initial 'th' ⟶

in words such as 'that', 'they', 'this' by the letter 'Ð' in upper case and by 'd' in lower case. This required casting new types that were used first in his *English Grammar* (1633; 2nd ed., 1634) and later in his other books, including *The Principles of Musik*.

But did students find it difficult to read the orthography in Butler's book? Fortunately, one answer appears in the autobiography, *Notes of Me*, by Roger North (1651–1734). North was initiated in music by the English composer John Jenkins (1592–1678); when he was about nine, Jenkins lent him his own copy of Butler's book, commending it as 'the best' of its kind. North studied the book 'not without difficulty' because of the different characters used in the text, such as 'de, for the, and dat for that'. But he mastered the task, and in *The Musicall Grammarian* (1728) he wrote that his intention was not to explain 'comon grammer [*sic*], for that is not wanted, nor ever will be, so long as Mr. Butler's excellent tract is extant'.

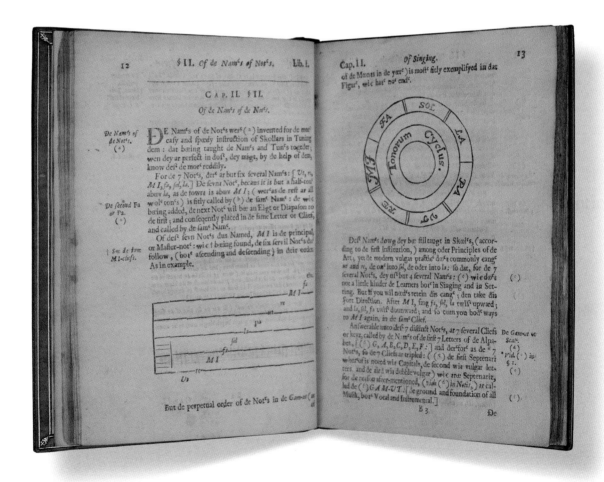

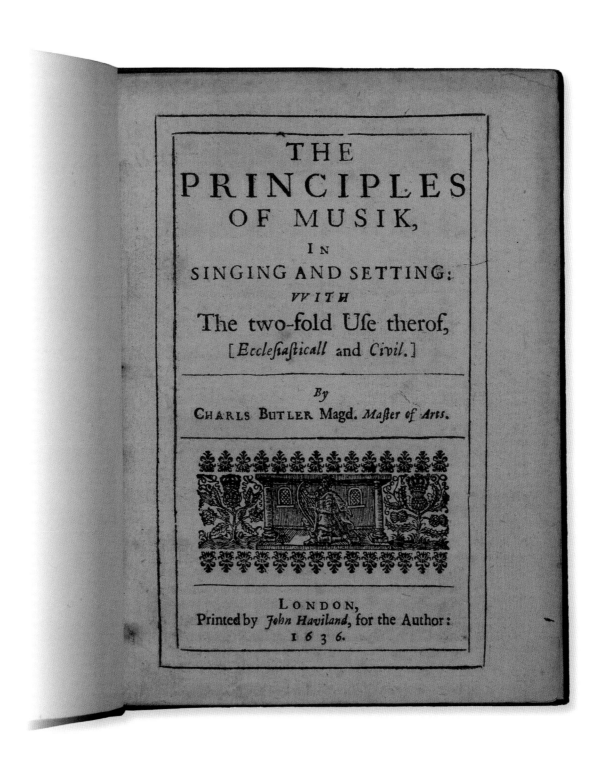

THE
PRINCIPLES
OF MUSIK,
IN
SINGING AND SETTING:
VVITH
The two-fold Uſe therof,
[Ecclesiasticall and Civil.]

By
CHARLS BUTLER Magd. Maſter of Arts.

LONDON,
Printed by John Haviland, for the Author:
1 6 3 6.

René Descartes (1596–1650)

Renatus Descartes Excellent Compendium of Music: With Necessary and Judicious Animadversions Thereupon by a Person of Honour

London: Printed by Thomas Harper, for Humphrey Moseley and Thomas Heath, 1653

The French philosopher and mathematician René Descartes is known for his explanation of the physical world by means of a continuum hypothesis in which space is identified with matter and the propagation of all action is by contact between particles of matter. Since his hypothesis used no explanatory principles other than concepts employed in mechanics, Descartes was the among the first to pursue what came to be called 'the mechanical philosophy'. However, there is no hint of this philosophy in the *Excellent Compendium*, which was written during 1618, when he was serving in the army of Prince Maurice of Nassau. The work was completed in December, and Descartes gave it to his friend, the Dutch scholar Isaac Beeckman (1588–1637), on 1 January 1619. Shortly after Descartes' death in 1650, it was published in Latin as *Compendium musicae*.

Early in the work, Descartes points out that there are two principal attributes of sound, its duration and pitch, all else from 'the Argument of Physiologists' (that is, physicists) being excluded. His aim was to establish an absolute, measurable guarantee for the veracity of the sense of hearing and for the ease in which it distinguishes certain consonant intervals. He found this guarantee in a treatise by the Renaissance music theorist Gioseffo Zarlino (1517–1590), who promulgated a variant of the ancient harmonic theory of the Pythagoreans. According to this variant, consonant intervals are obtained by dividing the string of a monochord into six parts—the so-called *senario*—instead of four.

Two other authors, both anonymous, contributed to the English translation. The first, named only as 'The Stationer', provided the rather florid introductory essay, in which he asks what it means to acquire the attributes of 'a complete Musition', defined as one who has 'swallowed' not only all of music theory but also '*Humane Learning*'. He claims that the latter consists of ten 'occupations', of which the first—that of a 'Physiologist'—is able to demonstrate the generation, nature, properties and effects of a 'natural' sound. He also made clear that he '*Midwiv'd*' the book 'into this our *English* World' and noted that the source for his translation had many '*grosse* Defects'. This suggests that his source was a manuscript now in the British Library, and that 'The Stationer' himself was its editor.

Recently discovered data in the Stationers' Company Archive establishes that 'The Stationer' was the physician and natural philosopher Walter Charleton (1619–1707). In 1654, Charleton published a book entitled *Physiologia*, in which he presented a translation and his own extension of a book written in 1649 by the French natural philosopher Pierre Gassendi (1592–1655). Drawing upon ideas of the ancient Epicureans, Gassendi had introduced a mechanical philosophy different from that of Descartes, for it relied on an emission hypothesis, according to which the physical world consists of very small spaces not filled by any body, together with very small bodies (material atoms) that have no empty space within them. Variants of this theory became common in England during the second half of the seventeenth century.

In *Physiologia*, Charleton devoted a section 'to that no less Erudite, than Noble Author of the *Animadversions on Descartes Musick Compendium*, the Lord *Viscount Brouncker*' (1620–1684) of Castle Lyons, Ireland. For many years, it has been claimed that Brouncker edited the *Compendium* translation, but this attribution can

no longer be maintained. His contribution consisted chiefly of numbered notes; the numbers, but not the notes, also appeared in the margins of the translation. Against Descartes, Brouncker argued that 'by the *Sense of Hearing*, wee doe judge of *Sounds* according to the *Geometrical*, not Arithmetical Proportion, or proportional *Division* of the *Strings* that give them'. To accomplish such divisions, he used the ancient geometrical methods of Euclid's canon of mean proportionals, as well as algebraic and logarithmic methods. He also included, for the first time, a logarithmically determined equal temperament, in opposition to Descartes' arithmetically determined just intonation.

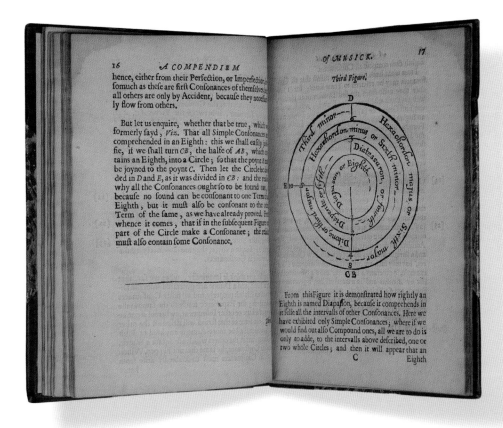

RENATUS DES-CARTES.

EXCELLENT

COMPENDIUM

OF

MUSICK:

WITH

Necessary and Judicious

ANIMADVERSIONS

Thereupon.

By a Person of HONOUR. *My Ld Brunkar*

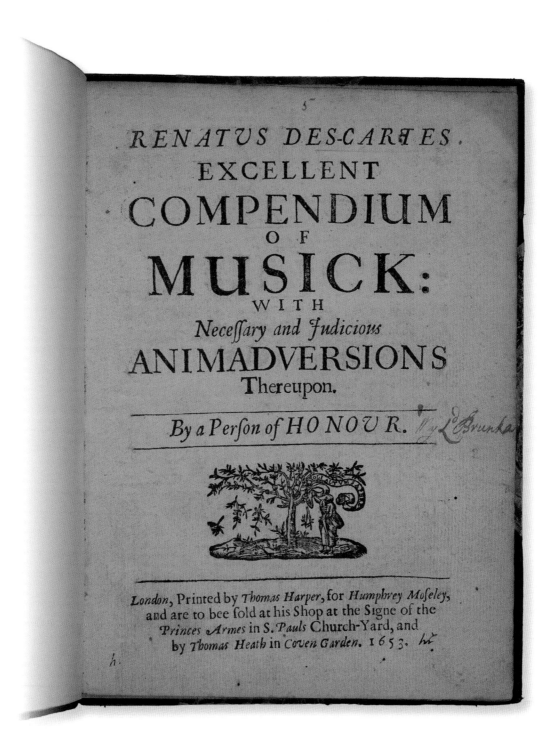

London, Printed by *Thomas Harper*, for *Humphrey Moseley*,
and are to bee sold at his Shop at the Signe of the
Princes Armes in S. *Pauls* Church-Yard, and
by *Thomas Heath* in *Coven Garden*. 1653.

Francis North, later 1st Baron Guilford (1637–1685)

A Philosophical Essay of Musick Directed to a Friend

London: Printed for John Martyn, Printer to the Royal Society, 1677

The English lawyer Francis North was born at Kirtling, Cambridgeshire, the country estate of his grandfather, Dudley, 3rd Lord North. Having dissipated the family fortune, he required that his eldest son, Dudley, and his family live at Kirtling Hall, extracting from them more than a fair cost for lodging, an arrangement that was difficult not only for Sir Dudley but also for Francis. As an infant, Francis was 'a nimble bright spark' and showed signs of independence, behaviour that irritated the controlling patriarch, so that at about the age of six he was sent to a small infant school run by 'a rigid presbisterian [*sic*]'. About four years later, he was transferred to a school in Bury St Edmunds, later known as the King Edward VI free grammar school.

On 8 June 1653, aged 15, Francis North entered St John's College, Cambridge, as a fellow-commoner under Thomas Frost (d.1674), a former pupil of the school at Bury and a graduate of St John's College who between 1649 and 1656 was a fellow of Trinity Hall. Here, North applied himself to music, including practice on the bass viol played either as a lyra viol (which is plucked and held across the knees) or as a division viol (which is bowed and held between the knees). He probably was instructed by the Cambridge musician John Lilly (d.1678), a theorbo and division viol player, who later became one of the resident musicians at Kirtling. Lilly afterwards moved to London where North became his patron and helped to support his large family.

Music was not North's sole study at Cambridge, for he was tutored in mathematics and in moral, natural and experimental philosophy by Edmund Matthews (d.1689), a fellow at Sidney Sussex College. Little is known about Matthews, who seems to have had a wide range of interests, including music. It is likely that seeds sown then bore fruit many years later in North's *Essay*.

On 17 November 1655, North left Cambridge without a degree to begin his legal education at the Middle Temple, where he was called to the bar (18 June 1661) and elected a bencher (5 June 1668). Thereafter, he rose rapidly in his profession, becoming chief justice of the Common Pleas (23 January 1675) and Lord Keeper of the Great Seal in 1682. North had been a protégé of Heneage Finch (1621–1682, from 1681 1st Earl of Nottingham), and like him was a learned lawyer of the royalist type.

In his brief but fecund *Essay*, North links for the first time the physics of sound, later called 'acoustics', with the newly emerging system of music, which in 1830 was given the name 'tonality'. Written shortly before his appointment as chief justice, it was licensed on 3 February 1677 and published anonymously. Extant copies indicate that there were two printings, the first of which contained errors that were corrected in the second printing, as in the copy shown overleaf. →

A
Philofophical
ESSAY
OF
MUSICK
Directed to a
FRIEND.

Feb. 3d
167⅗

Imprimatur,

Guil. Sill.

LONDON,
Printed for *John Martyn,* Printer to the Royal
Society ; at the *Bell* in Saint *Paul's*
Church-Yard, 1677.

After an introduction in the form of a letter to an anonymous friend, the main text is divided into nine sections. The first five sections are devoted to the physics of sound, including musical sound. They provide the rationale for the last four sections, where North enters as 'a *Philosopher*, to show what is allowable Musick, in order to make the Reasons upon which their Rules are founded understood'.

Section 1 provides a hypothesis concerning the production of sound in general by defining sound as a succession of short, sharp impulses produced when a deformable material medium is compressed and springs back, causing an internal motion ('tremble') that propagates through the medium to the ear. North then extends this hypothesis to include the concept of periodicity, defining tone in section 2 as a simple pendular vibration whose periods vibrate in equal intervals of time, i.e., they are isochronous. Without this principle, there would be no correlation between pitch and frequency ('timing').

Section 3 concerns the relation of tones in the musical scale as determined by a new theory of consonance as the sensory perception of periodic pulse fronts in the air. If these 'Pulses of *tones* are coincident one with the other, there is an Union of the sounds', i.e. two or more tones co-exist in the ear. Hence, the ratios that determine consonant intervals are found in the physical relations that exist in the resonance of elastic bodies. Section 4, on the production of musical-instrument tones, contains a new explanation of overblown tones produced when an air column in a trumpet segments ('breaks') into aliquot parts, each vibrating at a frequency proportionate to a tone's fundamental frequency.

Section 5 treats 'the varying and breaking of tones' and leads to a new definition of tone as a compound of simple pendular vibrations, each segment of which moves as a simple pendulum so that the stretched musical string vibrates simultaneously in a number of modes. Two experiments are described which demonstrate that there is a connection between nodes ('points') of absolute or comparative rest in a vibrating body, and that the higher modes of a string vibrations segment into what now are called partial tones (numbered 2 to 6) above a fundamental tone (1).

For sections 3 and 5 North created a 'Scheme' represented by two graphs showing periodicity patterns of the pulses in relation to their fundamental tone as a function of time. One graph shows the relative perfection of consonances including the importance of the bass, the identity of octaves and the function of consonant notes above a fundamental bass. The other graph shows the fundamental tone as the norm with which the pulses coincide and are heard as a simultaneous set of partial tones above a fundamental bass. These graphs represent the beginning of the formalisation of the system later known as tonality.

In April 1677, North's elder brother John, soon to become master of Trinity College, Cambridge, gave a copy of the Essay to Isaac Newton without revealing the author's name. On 21 April 1677, Newton responded in a letter in which he described the 'discours…about breaking of Tones into higher notes' as 'very ingenious & judicious' but commented 'I want experience to discern whether [it is] altogether solid'. (This letter was unknown until 1869, when it first appeared in print.)

John Christopher Pepusch (1667–1752)

A Treatise on Harmony: Containing the Chief Rules for Composing in Two, Three, and Four Parts

London: Printed by William Pearson, 2nd ed., 1731

Born in Berlin, Johann Christoph Pepusch came to London in 1688 and spent the rest of his life there, becoming one of its most important teachers of music in the first half of the eighteenth century. He was awarded the degree Doctor of Music by the University of Oxford in 1713. In 1725, he was one of the founding members of the Academy of Vocal Music, a group of musicians that studied and performed music composed after 1600. In 1731, it was renamed the Academy of Ancient Music, and in the following year Pepusch commenced giving lessons there to young boys. After his appointment in 1737 as organist of the Charterhouse School, he taught some of its students how to sing. In addition, he taught privately members of the nobility and gentry, as well as adult professional musicians. He also wrote several didactic works on music, which were published anonymously.

The *Treatise on Harmony* in its revised and enlarged 1731 edition is his most important theoretical work. According to his friend, the music historian Sir John Hawkins (1719–1789), the first edition (1730) was written by Pepusch's pupil and later patron James Hamilton, Lord Paisley (1686–1744, later 7th Earl of Abercorn), who entered it at Stationers' Hall; but there is insufficient evidence for this claim. Instead, it seems more likely that, owing to Pepusch's difficulties in writing correct English, Paisley edited the text. The 1731 second edition, intended

for more advanced students, contains an introduction and ten chapters that offered a range of subjects suited to forming a composer: plain counterpoint, modes, figurate counterpoint, discords, cadences, modulation, solmisation, transposition and canons, fugues and imitations.

Pepusch then began to study 'ancient' (Greek and Roman) theories of music, on the assumption that they might help advance music theory. Because aspects of his study involved mathematics, he consulted friends who were leading mathematicians: for example, Abraham De Moivre (1667–1754), Brook Taylor (1685–1731) and George Lewis Scott (1708–1780), the last of whom was a pupil of both Pepusch and De Moivre. All these men were Fellows of the Royal Society, as was Lord Paisley; and in 1745, Pepusch was also elected a Fellow. In 1746, he summarised some results of his studies in a paper published in the Royal Society's *Philosophical Transactions*.

Pepusch remained director of the Academy of Ancient Music until his death. During his lifetime, he amassed a large library of books, manuscripts and music that was one of the most notable private collections of his day. After his death, part of his library went to the British Museum, to which some items bearing Pepusch's ownership signature were later given by Hawkins. In July 1766, other parts of the collection were sold by auction and, unfortunately, dispersed.

A Treatise on Harmony:

CONTAINING

The Chief *Rules* for *Composing* in *Two, Three,* and *Four Parts.*

DEDICATED

To all Lovers of MUSICK,

By an *Admirer* of this AGREEABLE SCIENCE.

The Second Edition, *Alter'd, Enlarg'd,* and *Illustrated* by Examples in NOTES.

—— *Si quid noviſti, Rectius iſtis ;*
Candidus imperti : Si non, his utere mecum.

Hor. Epiſt.

LONDON Printed by *W. Pearſor,* 1731.　　10-6

Alexander van Haecken (1701–1757)

Portrait of Johannes Christophorus Pepusch

mezzotint, late 1730s

Alexander van Haecken was born in Antwerp, Belgium, and lived in London from the 1720s. His engraving of the composer and theorist John Christopher Pepusch (1667–1752) was based on an oil painting by Thomas Hudson (1701–1779), which is now in the National Portrait Gallery, London.

The art historian John F. Kerslake describes Hudson's portrait as showing 'dark blue eyes, pale brown arched eyebrows, cleft chin, wig falling behind shoulders, oyster-grey brocaded gown lined with crimson (gown of Mus.Doc. Oxford), white cravat and wrist ruffles'. According to Kerslake, the wig suggests a 1730s date for this painting, and the van Haecken engraving seems to have been made shortly thereafter.

Thos Hudson Pinxit.

A. Van Haecken fecit.

Iohannes Christophorus Pepusch.

Mus : Doct : Oxon.

John Holden (1729–1772)

An Essay towards a Rational System of Music

Glasgow: Printed for the author; London: Sold by R. Baldwin, 1770

The Englishman John Holden moved to Glasgow in the 1750s, where he set up shop as a merchant potter. He supplemented his activities by teaching music, writing and mathematics, playing the municipal carillon and copying university diplomas. From 1765, he directed church music at the college chapel of the University of Glasgow, where he became acquainted with Thomas Reid (1710–1796), Professor of Moral Philosophy. In 1766, Holden published by subscription the first of two parts of this *Essay*, announcing that he had put it to press 'sometime ago' and that it contained a sketch of a theory of music 'upon principles in a great measure new'. The full first edition was published in 1770, in two states (the second of which is seen here) that differ only in colophon and dedication. (The colophon of the first state reads 'Glasgow: Printed by Robert Urie, for the author'.)

In the first part of the *Essay*, Holden derives his principles for the practice of music from two 'natural' propensities of the human mind. Consciousness concerns the existence of the mind and its actual feelings; it relies solely on the senses and on custom. Common sense gives assurance of truths such as 'whatever has a beginning has a cause'; it relies not only on the senses but also on memory, so that from experiencing and remembering the existence of one thing, we intuitively include the existence of another. The two propensities, therefore, are sources of evidence, which, to be admissible, must be improved by experience.

In the second part, Holden summarises current knowledge about the theory of sound, including harmonics, sound perception, the co-vibration of particles and difference tones. In the eighteenth century, difference tones were called 'grave harmonics'. Not until the late nineteenth century were they understood as what was heard when two loud notes are sounded, the tone's frequency being the difference of the frequencies of those two notes.

Holden's *Essay* was the most important music treatise published in eighteenth-century Scotland. It is unique: no other music treatise of the time drew upon Scottish common sense philosophy, of which Thomas Reid was the leading representative. Reid's first book, *An Inquiry into the Human Mind*, was published in 1764. Although his subsequent books, which divided the mind into active and intellectual powers, did not appear until after Holden's death, Holden's description of the theory of musical practice as active and the theory of sound as intellectual appears to have been influenced by Reid's ideas.

Holden's *Essay* was frequently reprinted between 1775 and 1807.

AN

ESSAY

TOWARDS A

RATIONAL SYSTEM of MUSIC.

By JOHN HOLDEN.

Farlow

———— Mufic ————
To which refpondent fhakes the varied foul.   THOMSON.

Entered in Stationers-Hall.

GLASGOW:
Printed for the AUTHOR.
LONDON:
Sold by R. BALDWIN, in *Pater-Nofter-Row.*   MDCCLXX.
[PRICE 7s 6d. half bound.]

Augustus Frederic Christopher Kollmann (1756–1829)

A New Theory of Musical Harmony

London: Printed by W. Bulmer and Co. for the author, 1806

The music theorist A.F.C. Kollmann was born in the Electorate of Hannover, a kingdom within Germany whose prince acceded to the throne of Great Britain in 1714 as King George I. Although separately governed, Hannover and Great Britain remained in 'personal union'—they shared the same sovereign—until 1837, when Victoria became queen of Great Britain, as the Salic Law required that its ruler be a male successor of the royal family.

Kollmann was educated in Hannover and worked as an organist and schoolmaster there until 1782 when, in response to a command from King George III, he was selected to serve as organist and schoolmaster at the Royal German Chapel in St James's Palace, London, where he spent the rest of his life. He is remembered today for his efforts to give English readers knowledge of Johann Sebastian Bach (1685–1750) and his music, which included the first publication anywhere, in 1799, of several of Bach's compositions, and for his development of a new, generative theory of Western music—the system now called 'tonality'—in which 'every note, that is useful in music' obtained 'as positive a rule, as it denotes a positive sound'.

The music vignette printed on the title page of this book illustrates Kollmann's 'New Theory'. The bottom two staves, displaying a melody and bass, represent an axiom of the system: they indicate a C-major chord (a fundamental concord) followed by a dominant-seventh chord (with notes G-B-D-F, a fundamental discord) followed by another C-major chord. The four staves above the bottom two show how the melody can be transformed by successively introducing diatonic and chromatic 'passing notes'. The time signatures and bar lines in the vignette signify that Kollmann's theory accounted for musical rhythm (measure accents and beat accents) in addition to note successions and note simultaneities.

Kollmann dedicated his *New Theory* to the president (Sir Joseph Banks, 1743–1820) and council of the Royal Society of London. He engaged William Bulmer (1757–1830), printer of the society's *Philosophical Transactions*, to publish the textual component of the book (36 pages of music examples issued with the text were engraved by someone else). Although the vignette looks as if it were printed from an engraved plate, no plate marks are visible on the title page, and it appears that Bulmer solved the problem of printing letterpress text and engraved music on the same page by having the engraved music pressed onto a metal block which, after etching, was positioned into a frame called a forme, from which the whole title page was printed in a single impression.

Kollmann continued to develop his 'New Theory', and in 1823 issued a 'second edition, with considerable improvements'.

A

NEW THEORY

OF

MUSICAL HARMONY,

ACCORDING TO A COMPLETE AND NATURAL

SYSTEM OF THAT SCIENCE.

BY

AUGUSTUS FREDERICK CHRISTOPHER KOLLMANN,

ORGANIST OF HIS MAJESTY'S GERMAN CHAPEL AT ST. JAMES'S.

page 81.

LONDON:

PRINTED BY W. BULMER AND CO. CLEVELAND ROW,

FOR THE AUTHOR, (FRIARY, ST. JAMES'S PALACE), AND TO BE HAD OF HIM,

AND ALL THE PRINCIPAL MUSICSELLERS AND BOOKSELLERS.

PRICE A GUINEA AND A HALF.

Entered at Stationers' Hall.

1806.

Secrets

NATURAL MAGICK

John Baptista Porta,

A NEOPOLITANE.

IN TWENTY BOOKS

Wherein are set forth

All the RICHES and DELIGHTS.

Of the

NATURAL SCIENCES.

Giambattista Della Porta (1535–1615)

Natural Magick, in Twenty Books Wherein Are Set Forth All the Riches and Delights of the Natural Sciences

London: Printed for John Wright, 1669

Giambattista Della Porta was born in Vico Equense, Italy, and lived in Naples for much of his life. His publications included 17 plays, but today he is chiefly remembered for his works on cryptography and various scientific topics.

Natural Magick—the phrase refers to physical acts, not to the summoning of spirits (sorcery)—is the English translation of the title of the second, greatly expanded edition of Porta's *Magiae naturalis*, written in Latin and published in Naples in 1589. The first edition had been published there in 1558. About 1580, Porta established in his home the *Academia Secretorum Naturae* (Academy of the Secrets of Nature). The conversations and related experiments conducted at the academy led him to produce the second edition of his book. Republished several times in Naples and elsewhere, it appears to have reached a wide audience and become Porta's best-known work, forming the basis of his reputation.

The first English translation of the second Latin edition—the translator's name is not known—had been printed for the London booksellers Thomas Young and Samuel Speed in 1658. The 1669 edition featured here was printed from the same plates as the earlier edition, but with the title page updated to identify the new bookseller.

The 20 books that constitute the single volume of *Natural Magick* treat diverse topics, including the generation of animals, the production of new plants, counterfeiting gold, beautifying women, cookery and invisible writing. Music is discussed in several places. In Chapter 4 of Book 15, titled 'What noises will allure birds', Porta reports that 'the dolphin loves the harp', 'horses delight in the musick of the flute', and so on. In Chapter 2 of Book 19, titled 'Of instruments musical made with water', he describes how blowing a pipe into bubbling water can produce different tones.

Book 20 was called 'Of the Chaos' because the 'experiments' described there are so diverse that they could not fit within a single subject. In its Chapter 7, titled 'Of the harp and many wonderful properties thereof', Porta claims that 'all things living are charmed by musick' and records what ancient thinkers such as Plutarch, Pythagoras and Aristotle said about this. He adds that bears can be driven away by a drum, deaf people may be cured by a trumpet and madmen can be cured by hearing musical tunes. He notes that a harp that is played on will cause (by means of sympathetic vibration) another nearby harp to sound (if both have been strung to the same height).

Porta's concept of natural magic is based upon Hermetic and Neoplatonic traditions that were rife in Renaissance philosophy. According to these traditions, nature is an orderly and rational universe into which a magician- ⟶

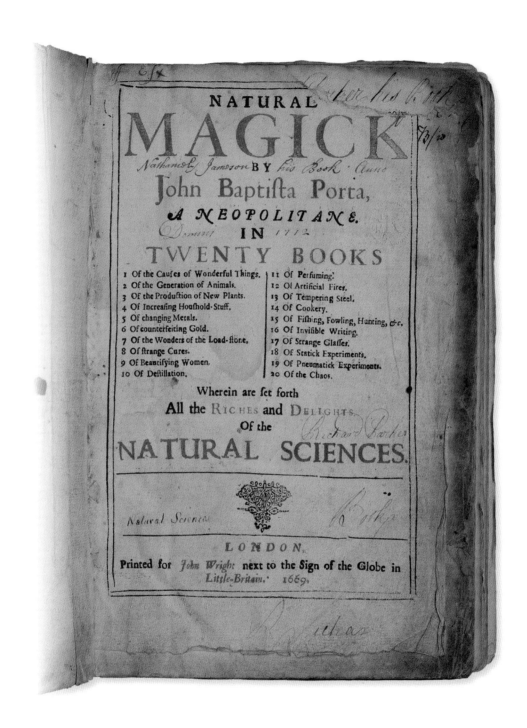

NATURAL

MAGICK

BY

John Baptista Porta,

A NEOPOLITANE.

IN

TWENTY BOOKS

1 Of the Causes of Wonderful Things.
2 Of the Generation of Animals.
3 Of the Production of New Plants.
4 Of Increasing Houshold-Stuff.
5 Of changing Metals.
6 Of counterfeiting Gold.
7 Of the Wonders of the Load-stone.
8 Of strange Cures.
9 Of Beautifying Women.
10 Of Destillation.
11 Of Perfuming.
12 Of Artificial Fires.
13 Of Tempering Steel.
14 Of Cookery.
15 Of Fishing, Fowling, Hunting, &c.
16 Of Invisible Writing.
17 Of Strange Glasses.
18 Of Statick Experiments.
19 Of Pneumatick Experiments.
20 Of the Chaos.

Wherein are set forth

All the RICHES and DELIGHTS.

Of the

NATURAL SCIENCES.

LONDON.

Printed for *John Wright* next to the Sign of the Globe in
Little-Britain. 1669.

scientist has insights revealed to him. His books were controversial in Italy and attracted the attention of the Inquisition, which prohibited their publication between 1592 and 1598.

The book has been well used over the centuries: it retains many doodles, inscriptions, marks of ownership and instances of censorship. Some of its eighteenth-century owners were likely young male students, who have written their names in the book, some several times, and presumably the year each acquired it. The schoolboy humour includes an example of mirror writing on the rear endpaper. When reversed, it reads: 'are not you a folish [*sic*] ass that cannot reed [*sic*] without a glass'.

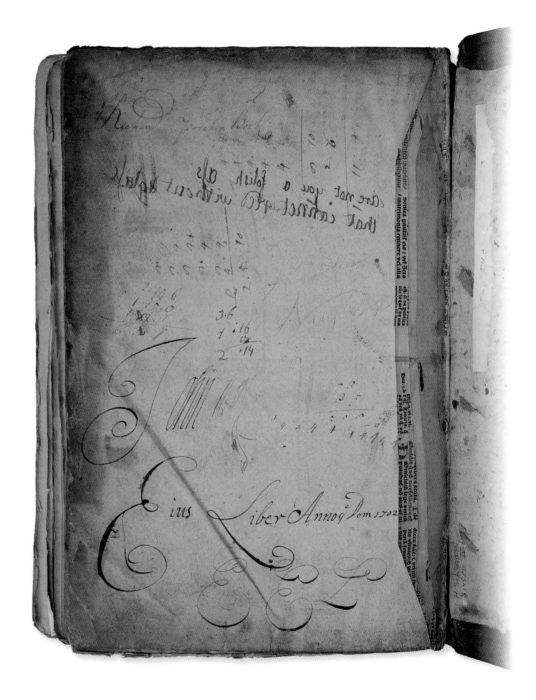

John Wilkins (1614–1672)

Mercury: or the Secret and Swift Messenger. Shewing, How a Man May with Privacy and Speed Communicate His Thoughts to a Friend at Any Distance

London: Printed for Rich[ard] Baldwin, near the Oxford-Arms in Warwick-lane, 2nd ed., 1694

The theologian and philosopher Reverend Dr John Wilkins wrote a number of popularisations of science which helped to bring about the 'scientific revolution'— the establishment of a mechanistic concept of nature based upon the findings of science. As a central figure in this movement for intellectual reform, Wilkins became a target of criticism, and his popularisations were attacked both by scientific conservatives and by those who viewed the new science as a threat to classical learning and the authority of Holy Scripture. However, in the face of bitter ideological, social and political conflicts, he seems to have had a unique talent for enlisting friendly cooperation from the best brains of his day.

Mercury was first published in 1641, the second 1694 edition (shown here) was reissued in 1695 and a third edition appeared in 1707. The book has been described as the most important early English work on cryptology, as it contains valuable information concerning methods of secret writing, secret speech, secret gestures and codebreaking. Besides giving a long list of historical devices used for concealing messages, Wilkins describes ways in which items such as musical notes, stamps and playing cards have been used for that purpose.

Chapter XVIII of *Mercury* is entitled 'Concerning a Language that may consist only of Tunes and Musical Notes, without any articulate sound'. If musical notes are used for this purpose, not only according to 'their different *Tones* but their *Times* also', then may 'each Letter of the Alphabet be rendred by a single sound'. Here Wilkins cites *The Man in the Moone: or a Discourse of a Voyage Thither by Domingo Gonsales the Speedy Messenger* (1638), an anonymously published work by Francis Godwin (1562–1633), Bishop of Llandaff and Hereford, who had devised an alphabet of musical notes ostensibly for communication between Earth and inhabitants of the Moon.

Wilkins considered his system of musical tunes superior to Godwin's, and conjectured that the '*utterance* of these Musical tunes' could 'serve for the Universal Language, and the writing of them for the Universal Character'. Such a 'Universal Character' would benefit mankind, as it could express things and notions 'legible to all people and countries' and 'mightily conduct to the spreading and promoting of all arts and sciences'. He noted the advantage of a 'Universal Language' based upon music: it could be conveyed by trumpets, bells or drums over longer distances than was possible for speech. But when he published his *Essay towards a Real Character and a Philosophical Language* in 1668, no tunes or music notations ('characters') were mentioned.

That same year, Wilkins was appointed Bishop of Chester. It was the year of the plague, and his longtime friend, the polymath Robert Hooke (1635–1703), who had served as Wilkins' philosophical assistant in preparing his *Essay* for publication, moved from London and lived with him until Wilkins' death. Between 1673 and 1680, Hooke wrote numerous memoranda concerning a universal alphabet, character and language. Probably inspired by Wilkins, Hooke made several attempts to devise a new method of music notation, one of which used vowels, consonants and diphthongs in place of the common notation. This attempt is described in his 'Musick Scripts', a manuscript written between 1671 and 1676 that is preserved in the library of Trinity College, Cambridge.

Celebrated Scores

Matthew Locke (1621–1677)

Melothesia: or, Certain General Rules for Playing upon a Continued-Bass. With a Choice Collection of Lessons for the Harpsicord and Organ of All Sorts. The First Part

London: Printed for J. Carr, 1673

The organist and prolific composer Matthew Locke began his musical life as a choirboy in Exeter Cathedral, advancing to a grade intermediate between chorister and lay vicar. His activities during the English Civil War (1642–51) are not known. Although Exeter had declared for parliament, cathedral services seem to have resumed in September 1643, when the city again came under royalist control. It has been conjectured that Locke became acquainted with King Charles I, his wife and son during this period, but there is little evidence for this. He may have become a Catholic when he joined the exiled court at The Hague, returning to England in 1651. In 1655, he married the daughter of a Catholic.

In spite of religious and political differences during the time of the Commonwealth, Locke became friendly with the amateur musician Silas Taylor (1624–1678), a parliamentary sequestration commissioner in Hereford. Their long friendship is evident from Locke's gift of the manuscript of *Melothesia* to Taylor, who provided Locke with a house in Hereford and organised music meetings in which he took a leading part. There were suspicions that these meetings were pretexts for assemblies of Papists, and in 1654, Locke's own beliefs came under investigation.

In the mid-1650s, Locke moved to London, where he became involved in the musical dramas, the only form of public theatre permitted under the Commonwealth. During this period the composer Henry Purcell (1659–1695) was his closest friend. After the Restoration in 1660, King Charles II appointed Locke 'composer in ordinary'. From 1662 onwards, Locke served as organist of Queen Catherine's Catholic Chapel, and during the plague year of 1665, he accompanied the court to Oxford. His friends at the time included Roger L'Estrange (1616–1704), bass-viol player and court licenser of books, and Christopher Simpson (c.1602–1669), music theorist, composer and viol player.

Melothesia, which means 'the setting of melody', is the first English publication to describe a notation for playing music on an instrument capable of producing chords, such as a harpsichord or organ. The notation does not show all the notes to be played, but presents instead a 'continued bass' that indicates the composition's successive chordal structure. Performers have to improvise the notes they play, but they need to adhere to the presented structure. Locke provides ten rules that a performer should follow. No other English book on the subject appeared until 1705, when Gottfried Keller's *A Compleat Method for Attaining to Play Thorough Bass upon either Organ, Harpsicord or Theorbo-Lute* was published. (The term 'thorough bass' superseded the term 'continued bass', which derived from the Italian 'basso continuo'.)

→

Locke's book opens with two items printed in letterpress: a dedication to L'Estrange, followed by 'Advertisements to the Reader' which include the rules for playing a continued bass. Two engraved pages follow that provide musical examples of the 'Precepts in the Rules'. Next comes an advertisement for books, ruled papers, and music and musical instruments sold by the printer, followed by 83 pages of music by Locke, by seven other named composers and by various anonymous composers. These pages do not exemplify continued bass.

The music, printed on six-line staves, was engraved rather crudely on copperplates. Music types could not have been used to print this music as the stave portions of those types had five lines. Locke's book was reportedly the third English music book printed from engraved copperplates. Its engraver has not been identified, although it could have been Thomas Cross, who seems to have specialised in portraits but is known to have engraved some music in copper. His engraving skills were surpassed by his son, also named Thomas, who is estimated to have engraved in copper at least a third of all broadside ballads published in England before 1700.

Carr's printing shop was at the Middle Temple from about 1672 to 1695, but he removed to other addresses during the period when the Middle Temple was being rebuilt after the Great Fire of London in 1666. The second part of *Melothesia* was never published.

Henry Purcell (1659–1695)

Orpheus Britannicus: A Collection of All the Choicest Songs for One, Two, and Three Voices

London: Printed by William Pearson and sold by John Young, 2nd ed., 1706

Henry Purcell is renowned as a leading English composer of the Baroque period. His music, notably his opera *Dido and Aeneas*, composed in 1688, continues to be performed today. In 1679, Purcell was appointed organist of Westminster Abbey, where he is buried, and from 1682, he also served as organist of the Chapel Royal.

Orpheus Britannicus was dedicated to Purcell's pupil, the singer Lady Annabella Howard (née Dives, 1674–1728), by the composer's widow, Frances Purcell (d.1706). It was published posthumously in three editions. The first edition, although 'design'd to have been publish'd some considerable time before now' and for which subscriptions had been obtained, was printed in 1698 by John Heptinstall for the bookseller Henry Playford, who increased by more than 30 the number of Purcell songs initially planned for inclusion. In 1702, 'the second book' of *Orpheus Britannicus* 'which renders the First Compleat' was printed in London by William Pearson for Playford. A copy of it is bound with the book shown here. Finally, the second edition 'with large additions' was printed by Pearson for John Young in 1706 and sold also by John Cullen, whose catalogue of music for sale is printed in the book. All three editions include an engraving of Purcell by Robert White (1645–1703) after a portrait painted by John Closterman (1669–1711) shortly before Purcell's death.

Both the music type Heptinstall used to print the first edition in 1698 and the different music type used by Pearson to print the 1702 and 1706 editions exemplify the so-called 'new tied note'. As shown in the following example of Pearson's type, notes were cast with stems and angled beams so that successive quaver and semiquaver notes in a beat could be joined together.

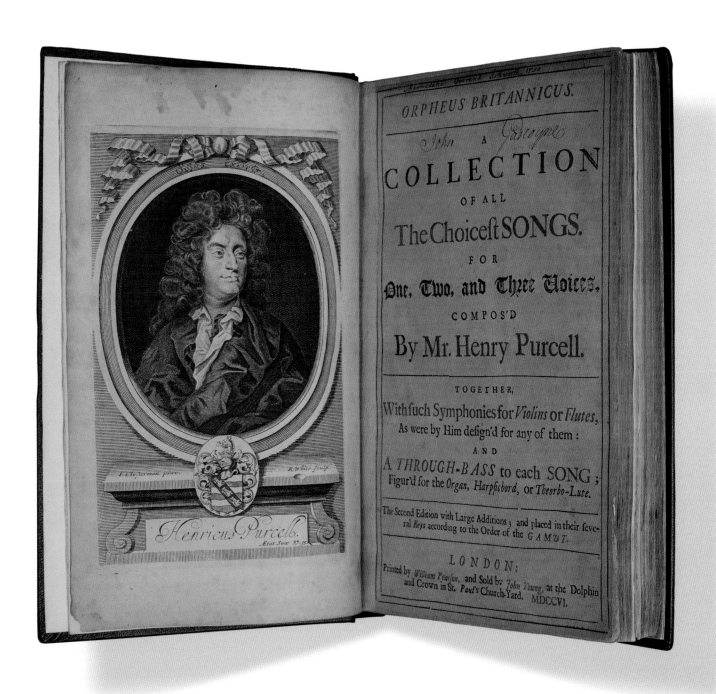

ORPHEUS BRITANNICUS.

A

COLLECTION

OF ALL

The Choiceſt SONGS.

FOR

One, Two, and Three Voices,

COMPOS'D

By Mr. Henry Purcell.

TOGETHER,

With ſuch Symphonies for *Violins* or *Flutes*,
As were by Him deſign'd for any of them :

AND

A *THROUGH-BASS* to each SONG ;
Figur'd for the *Organ, Harpſichord,* or *Theorbo-Lute.*

The Second Edition with Large Additions ; and placed in their ſeve-
ral *Keys* according to the Order of the *GAMUT.*

LONDON:

Printed by *William Pearſon,* and Sold by *John Young,* at the Dolphin
and Crown in St. *Paul's* Church-Yard, MDCCVI.

John Christopher Pepusch (composer, 1667–1752)
George Bickham (artist and engraver, c.1706–1771)

Alexis: A Cantata

London: T[homas] Cooper, 1738

John Christopher Pepusch's most famous cantata, *Alexis*, composed for voice and accompaniment (a continuo with figured bass) was initially published by John Walsh and Peter Randall in London in 1810, as number 2 of 'Six English Cantatas' that Pepusch dedicated to Jemima Grey (1675–1728), then Marchioness of Kent. In addition to his theoretical work, he wrote numerous compositions, including the overture to John Gay's ballad opera, *The Beggar's Opera*, which opened in London in 1728.

The edition featured here was advertised as published 'this day' in *The Country Journal, or The Craftsman* on 9 December 1738, and was subsequently reissued as number 10 of volume 2 of the collection called *Bickham's Musical Entertainer*. Each of this edition's four pages was printed on one side only. Above the engraved music is an etched vignette by George Bickham the Younger, who worked in London as a printmaker, publisher and picture framer.

Alexis was one of Pepusch's most popular works and continues to be performed and recorded.

Johann Sebastian Bach (1685–1750)

Preludes et Fugues pour le Forte-Piano, II. Partie

London: Printed by Broderip et Wilkinson, [1808]

The first English edition of the 48 preludes and fugues that comprise *The Well-Tempered Clavier (Books 1 and 2)*, one of the greatest works of renowned German Baroque composer Johann Sebastian Bach, was published in London by Broderip and Wilkinson in 1802. The work, often referred to simply as 'the 48', was not published in any printed form until well after Bach's death. This edition, containing 12 preludes and 12 fugues from part 2 of the '48', is extremely rare: only one copy is known to be extant.

No references to Bach appear to have been made in England during his lifetime, and British interest in him did not occur until about 1770, stimulated by the arrival in England of Germans with knowledge of him and his music. In *An Essay on Practical Musical Composition*, published in London in 1799, Augustus Frederic Christopher Kollmann said of the '48': 'This most ingenious, most learned, and yet practicable work, is so highly esteemed by all who can judge of it, that as it is grown scarce, I intend to offer it to the public analyzed'. Broderip and Wilkinson subscribed to Kollmann's treatise and presumably decided to publish their edition of part of the '48' before Kollmann had the opportunity to produce the work he had announced but never published.

The text of this Broderip and Wilkinson publication was copied from the edition of part 2 of the '48' issued by Nicolaus Simrock in Paris and Bonn in 1801. This accounts for the use of French on the title page and the dedication to the Conservatoire de Musique, established in Paris in 1795.

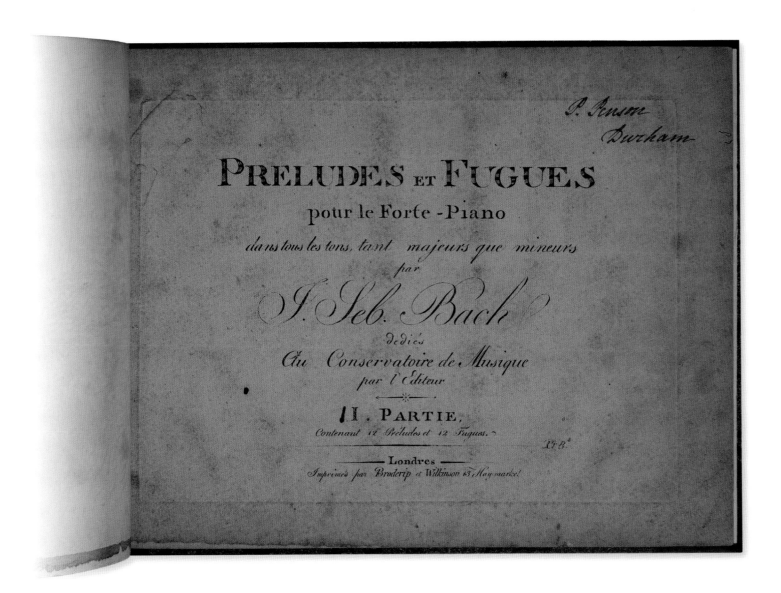

Published by National Library of Australia Publishing
Canberra ACT 2600

ISBN: 9781922507877

The National Library of Australia acknowledges Australia's First Nations Peoples—
the First Australians—as the Traditional Owners and Custodians of this land and
gives respect to the Elders—past and present—and through them to all Australian
Aboriginal and Torres Strait Islander people.

Rare Books and Music Curator: Dr Susannah Helman
Publisher: Lauren Smith
Managing editors: Amelia Hartney and Rosalind Clarke
Editor: Robert Nichols
Designer: Stan Lamond
Image coordinator: Madeleine Warburton
Proofreader: Mary Webb

Printed in Canberra, Australia, by CanPrint on FSC®-certified paper

Find out more about NLA Publishing at nla.gov.au/national-library-publishing.

A catalogue record for this book is available from the National Library of Australia.